GAME DAY
IOWA FOOTBALL

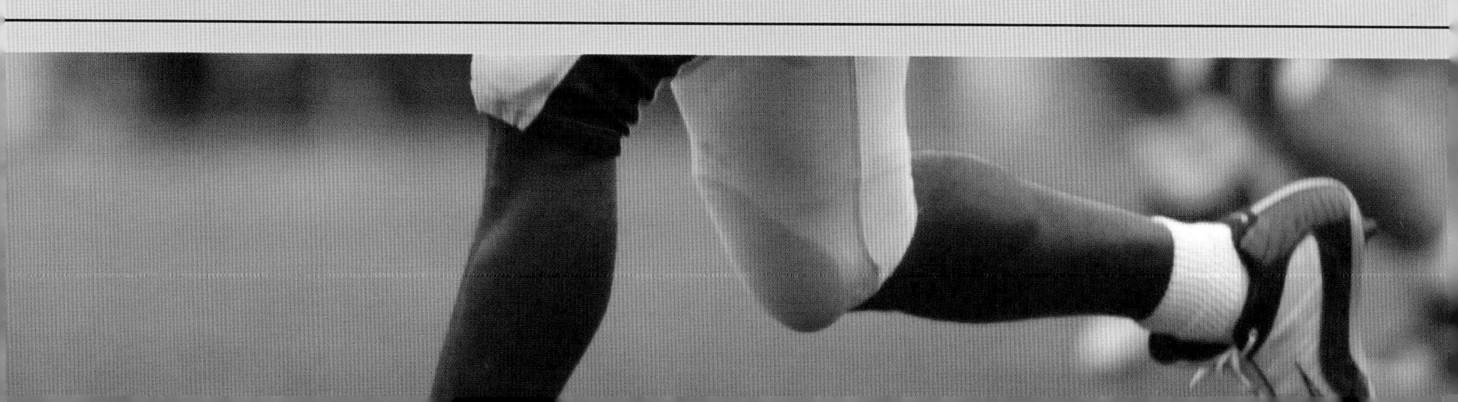

Chad Greenway

GAME DAY
IOWA FOOTBALL

The Greatest Games, Players, Coaches and Teams in the Glorious Tradition of Hawkeye Football

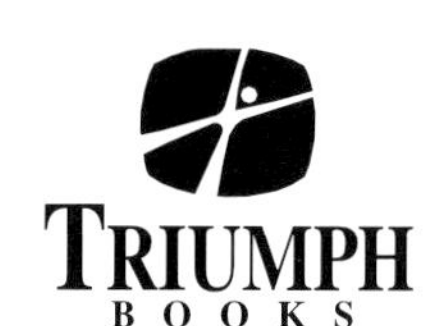

Library of Congress Control Number: 2007902502

This book is available in quantity at special discounts for your group or organization. For further information, contact:

Triumph Books
542 South Dearborn Street
Suite 750
Chicago, Illinois 60605
(312) 939-3330
Fax (312) 663-3557

CONTRIBUTING WRITER: Pat Harty

EDITOR: Rob Doster

PHOTO EDITOR: Tim Clark
ASSISTANT PHOTO EDITOR: Danny Murphy

DESIGN: Eileen Wagner
PRODUCTION: Patricia Frey

PHOTO CREDITS: Athlon Sports Archive, AP/Wide World Photos, University of Iowa-CMP Photo Service

Printed in China

ISBN: 978-1-60078-016-5

Contents

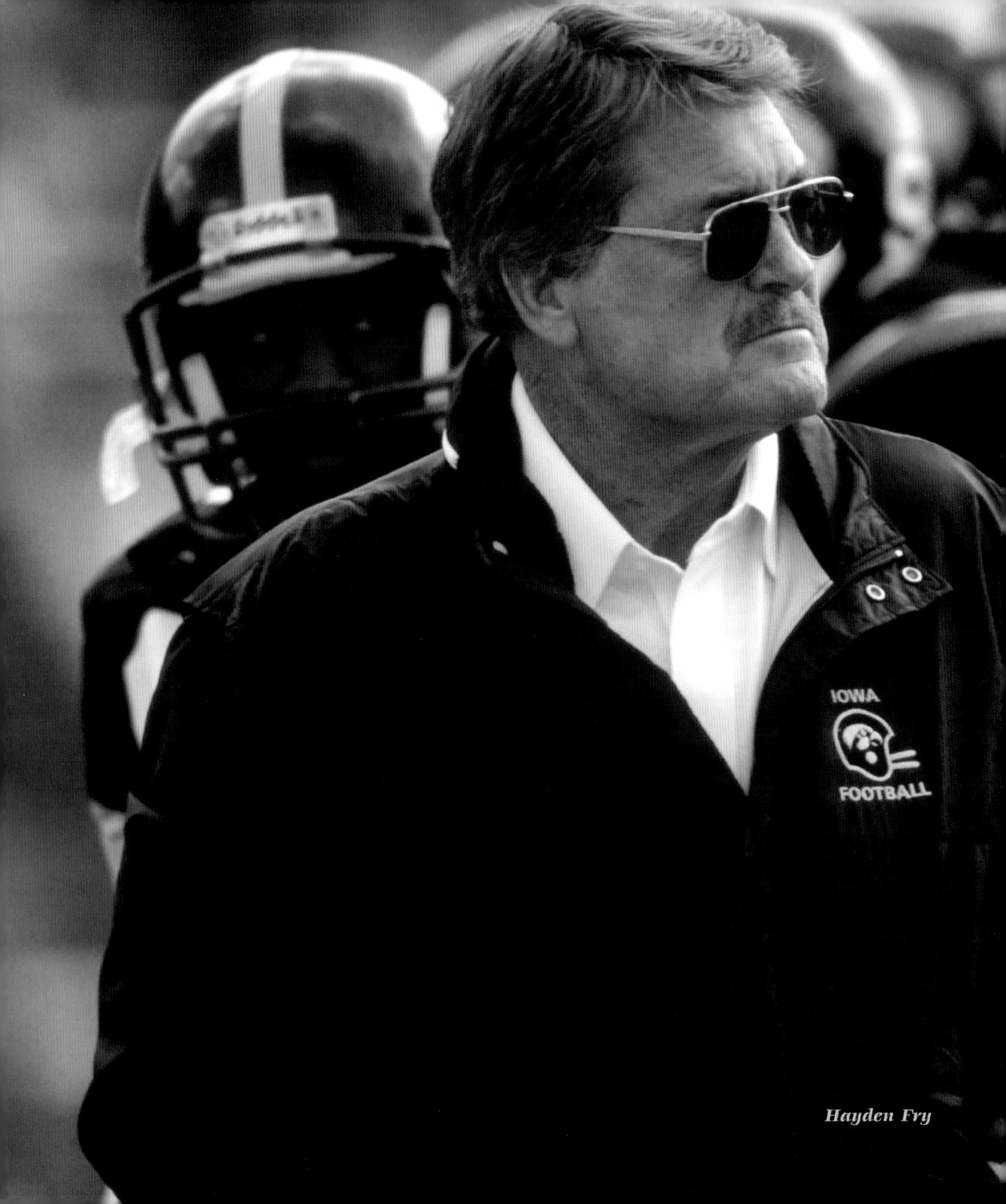

Hayden Fry

Foreword

Iowa football has been a big part of my life since 1978, the year I was offered the opportunity to coach the Hawkeyes. I had just finished my 15th season as a major college coach, the last six at North Texas State, and had received good job offers before, but the timing on this one was different.

We had just finished another excellent (9–2) season at North Texas but had not received a bowl bid. The past four years our teams had gone 32–12 with no bowl offers. We were tired of being rejected.

So I took the Iowa job offer to my coaches, who thought we should explore it. They knew the Big Ten champion was guaranteed a Rose Bowl berth, and a good season assured playing in a bowl game somewhere.

We did some research on the Hawkeyes and learned they hadn't had sustained success since the days of Coach Forest Evashevski in the 1950s and hadn't had a winning season in the past 17 years. We found that hard to understand. The Hawkeyes had strong financial support, played in a state without a major professional team and got tremendous coverage from the news media.

And we noticed something else. The previous season the Hawkeyes had won only two games, but in looking at films you could see that their games were well-attended. We wondered how Iowa fans would respond to really good teams.

After being assured that Iowa was committed to a successful football program, I accepted the job and moved with my North Texas coaching staff pretty much intact. It included Bill Brashier, Bill Snyder, Don Patterson, Clovis Hale and Howard Cissell. From the previous Iowa staff I retained Dan McCarney, Bernie Wyatt and Tom Cecchini, then hired a successful high school coach, Barry Alvarez.

They are the ones who worked long and hard to help me upgrade facilities and create a winning attitude. We had no timetable, but we were convinced we could give Hawkeye fans a winner. And three years later we did.

The 1981 season was our breakthrough. We beat UCLA and Nebraska, both ranked in the Top Ten, then earned a share of the Big Ten title and a Rose Bowl berth. That team is special because achievements far exceeded expectations. It proved Iowa football could produce champions, and it served as the cornerstone to my 20 years as Iowa's head football coach.

We had some wonderful teams during that time. Three of them won Big Ten championships; 14 played in bowl games. Many were ranked in the Top 20. The 1985 team made it all the way to No. 1. I cherish the memories they gave me.

Over the years, we recruited good young men who worked hard and succeeded in the classroom as well as on the field. I'm as proud of the degrees they earned as I am their success on the field. I'm proud of my coaches and players who have become top assistants and head coaches at other universities. I'm especially proud that one of them, Kirk Ferentz, has followed me so successfully at Iowa.

Since retirement in 1999, I've had several occasions to stand on the field at Kinnick Stadium and look around. I see more than 70,000 wonderful Hawkeye supporters—the greatest fans on earth—in one of the most historic stadiums in college football.

It's a wonderful experience and brings back a lot of great memories. It was a truly a privilege for me to be Iowa's football coach for 20 years.

—Hayden Fry

MONTGOMERY
41
KNIGHT
8
MULHERIN
29

Introduction

The images are unforgettable and too numerous to count.

Hayden Fry, stalking the sidelines in those distinctive sunglasses, restoring pride to the Hawkeye program with equal parts brashness, confidence and homespun charm. Nile Kinnick, inspiring a nation with his play on the field and his heroism off it. Chuck Long, setting new Big Ten standards for the passing game and coming just short of college football's ultimate individual award. A packed Kinnick Stadium giving full-throated support to the Hawkeyes. Championships won; legends created.

We're distilling the pageantry and drama of Iowa football into the pages that follow. It's a daunting task. Few college football programs in the country inspire the loyalty and passion that the Hawkeye football program exacts from its fans—and with good reason.

The numbers alone are impressive: 11 national award-winners, including the Heisman Trophy won by Nile Kinnick in 1939. Twelve inductees into the College Football Hall of Fame. Countless statistical milestones.

But numbers alone don't do justice to the greatness of Iowa football. With its commitment to excellence, the Hawkeye program has knit itself into the fabric of the entire state.

Hayden Fry encapsulated the personality of Iowa football upon accepting the job: "I have no time schedule on getting Iowa a winning football team. But I will tell you we will be competitive, tough and colorful. If I did not believe Iowa could win in the near future, I would not have left North Texas."

Mission accomplished.

Through the words and images we present, we hope we have captured the true flavor of Hawkeye football. Decades have passed since players first donned the black and gold, but one thing hasn't changed: Iowa football is an unmatched tradition, a legacy of greatness, a way of life in the Hawkeye State.

Dallas Clark

The Greatest Players

Iowa's roster of greats reads like a who's who of Big Ten legends. The names are familiar to fans of college football, and for the fans of the Hawkeyes' rivals, they still bring a shiver of dread.

Iowa has had so many great players that they can't all be included here, which is why the following list should be considered representative, not definitive.

We start with Iowa's greatest legend and its only Heisman Trophy winner.

NILE KINNICK

Halfback/defensive back
1937–1939

You could argue forever about who is the greatest player in school history, but there is no argument about who is the most famous and the most inspirational.

Nile Kinnick earned that distinction for how he played on the field, for how he lived off it and for how he died.

Kinnick captured the nation's attention by leading a lightly regarded Iowa squad to a 6–1–1 record as a senior in 1939. He helped establish his legend by leading Iowa to upset victories over Minnesota and Notre Dame in consecutive games.

Kinnick did everything for the Hawkeyes in 1939. He ran for touchdowns. He threw for touchdowns. He intercepted passes. He made PAT kicks. And he was among the nation's best punters.

Kinnick scored or passed for all but 23 of the points scored by the 1939 squad. He was second in the nation with eight interceptions and led the country with 377 kickoff return yards.

The handsome 5'8", 167-pound back was the heart and soul of Coach Eddie Anderson's Ironmen unit of 1939. He scored the Hawkeyes' only touchdown and converted the extra point in Iowa's 7–6 upset of Notre Dame. Kinnick also punted 16 times for 731 yards—both school records—in that game against the Irish.

According to one account of the winning touchdown, Kinnick was asked in the huddle, "Can you take it, Nile?" To which Kinnick responded, "I think I've got a couple of broken ribs on my right side, so let's run the play to the left side." True or not, the story epitomizes the legend of Nile Kinnick—his courage, his selflessness, his love for his team.

He won virtually every individual honor college football had to offer in 1939, becoming Iowa's only recipient of the Heisman Trophy in addition to grabbing the Camp and Maxwell Awards. To top it off, he also was named the nation's Outstanding Male Athlete for 1939, beating out baseball great Joe DiMaggio for the honor.

Kinnick gave up a chance to play professional football and enlisted in the Navy with the United States on the brink of entering World War II. He trained to be a fighter pilot.

Nile wrote a final letter to his parents before deploying with the U.S.S. *Lexington* in late May 1943. It read, in part: "The task which lies ahead is adventure as well as duty, and I am anxious to get at it. I feel better in mind and body than I have for 10 years and am quite certain I can meet the foe confident and unafraid. 'I have set the Lord always before me, because He is at my right hand. I shall not be moved.' Truly, we have shared to the full life, love and laughter. Comforted in the knowledge that your thought and prayer go with us every minute, and sure that your faith and courage will never falter, no matter the outcome, I bid you au revoir."

Days later, on June 2, 1943, he was killed in an airplane crash in the Caribbean Sea off the coast of Venezuela.

Iowa's stadium was named in Kinnick's honor in 1972—it's the country's only stadium named for a Heisman Trophy winner—and his jersey No. 24 is one of two retired numbers at Iowa.

©UNIVERSITY OF IOWA ~ CMP PHOTO SERVICE

NILE KINNICK'S HEISMAN TROPHY ACCEPTANCE SPEECH

Kinnick's speech, given about a year before the United States entered World War II, is remembered as one of the most eloquent and moving addresses ever given by a Heisman winner. AP reporter Whitney Martin wrote, "You realized the ovation (after his Heisman speech) wasn't alone for Nile Kinnick, the outstanding college football player of the year. It was also for Nile Kinnick, typifying everything admirable in American youth."

Here are his remarks that day:

"Thank you, very very kindly Mr Holcombe. It seems to me that everyone is letting their superlatives run away with them this evening, but none the less, I want you to know that I'm mighty, mighty happy to accept this trophy this evening.

"Every football player in the United States dreams about winning that trophy and of this fine trip to New York. Every player considers that trophy the acme in recognition of this kind. And the fact that I am actually receiving this trophy tonight almost overwhelms me, and I know that all of those boys who have gone before me must have felt somewhat the same way.

"From my own personal viewpoint, I consider my winning this award as indirectly a great tribute to the coaching staff at the University of Iowa, headed by Dr. Eddie Anderson, and to my teammates sitting back in Iowa City. A finer man and a better coach never hit these United States, and a finer bunch of boys never graced the gridirons of the Midwest, than that Iowa team in 1939. I wish that they might all be with me tonight to receive this trophy. They certainly deserve it.

"I want to take this grand opportunity to thank collectively, all the sportswriters and all the sportscasters, and all those who have seen fit, have seen their way clear to cast a ballot in my favor for this trophy. And I also want to take this opportunity to thank Mr. Prince and his committee, the Heisman award committee, and all those connected with the Downtown Athletic Club for this trophy, and for the fine time that they're showing me. And not only for that, but for making this fine and worthy trophy available to the football players of this country.

"Finally, if you will permit me, I'd like to make a comment which in my mind, is indicative, perhaps, of the greater significance of football, and sports emphasis in general in this country, and that is, I thank God I was warring on the gridirons of the Midwest, and not on the battlefields of Europe. I can speak confidently and positively that the players of this country, would much more, much rather struggle and fight to win the Heisman award, than the Croix de Guerre.

"Thank you."

AUBREY DEVINE

Halfback/defensive back
1919–1921

Before there was Nile Kinnick, there was Aubrey Devine. Devine thrilled Hawkeye fans in the early 1920s with his versatility and playmaking.

He was a three-time All-Big Ten selection and a consensus All-American in 1921 when he led Iowa to an undefeated season and the school's the first undisputed Big Ten title.

He dominated games from his halfback position much like Kinnick did nearly two decades after.

Devine's greatest performance arguably came against perennial power Minnesota on November 5, 1921. You name it and Devine did it for the Hawkeyes that day.

He scored four touchdowns and passed for two more while accumulating 464 total yards on rushes, passes and kick returns. He also kicked five extra points during Iowa's 41–7 victory in Minneapolis.

Minnesota coach Henry Williams, for whom the school's basketball arena is named, paid Devine the ultimate compliment afterward, saying "he was the greatest player who ever stepped on our field."

Devine was just as impressive during a victory against Iowa State in 1920. He dominated the game on both offense and defense. He had a stat line that included a rushing touchdown, a passing touchdown, three interceptions and two successful drop kicks.

Devine also beat Purdue with a dazzling punt return for a touchdown, but he told former Iowa sports information director George Wine that his favorite moment came when he drop-kicked a field goal in 1921 to end Notre Dame's 20-game winning streak by a 10–7 margin.

Howard Jones coached Devine at Iowa then went on to earn fame for turning Southern California into a national power. Jones mentored his share of great players at both schools, but Devine was special.

Jones called Devine "the greatest backfield man I have ever coached or seen in the modern era."

Devine rarely was taken out of game and he rarely got injured or threw an interception. He rushed for nearly 2,000 yards during his career and scored 161 points in 21 games.

Forty-nine years after his graduation from Iowa, Devine was named to the All-Time Hawkeye team, selected in conjunction with the Big Ten's 75th anniversary celebration in 1970. Devine died in 1981 in Escondido, California.

GORDON LOCKE

Fullback/defensive back
1920–1922

The driving force behind Iowa's undefeated season in 1922, Locke was a durable and powerful fullback. He carried the ball 430 times during three seasons of varsity competition, but was only thrown for 11 yards in losses.

The Denison, Iowa, native set a Big Ten record in 1922 that neither Red Grange nor Tom Harmon could equal by scoring 12 touchdowns in five conference games. Locke scored 32 touchdowns during his career, which still ranks among the best in school history.

He earned All-America honors in 1922 and was selected as a defensive back on Iowa's all-time football team.

A year earlier, Locke played a key role in the Hawkeyes' 10–7 upset of Notre Dame, scoring Iowa's only touchdown as the Irish focused on Iowa All-American Aubrey Devine. "We had heard so much about Devine, but the guy who hurt us the most that day was Locke," said Notre Dame Coach Knute Rockne.

During his three varsity seasons, the Hawkeyes posted a 19–2 record and were riding a 17-game winning streak when he graduated. Locke turned a law degree into a successful practice in Washington, D.C.

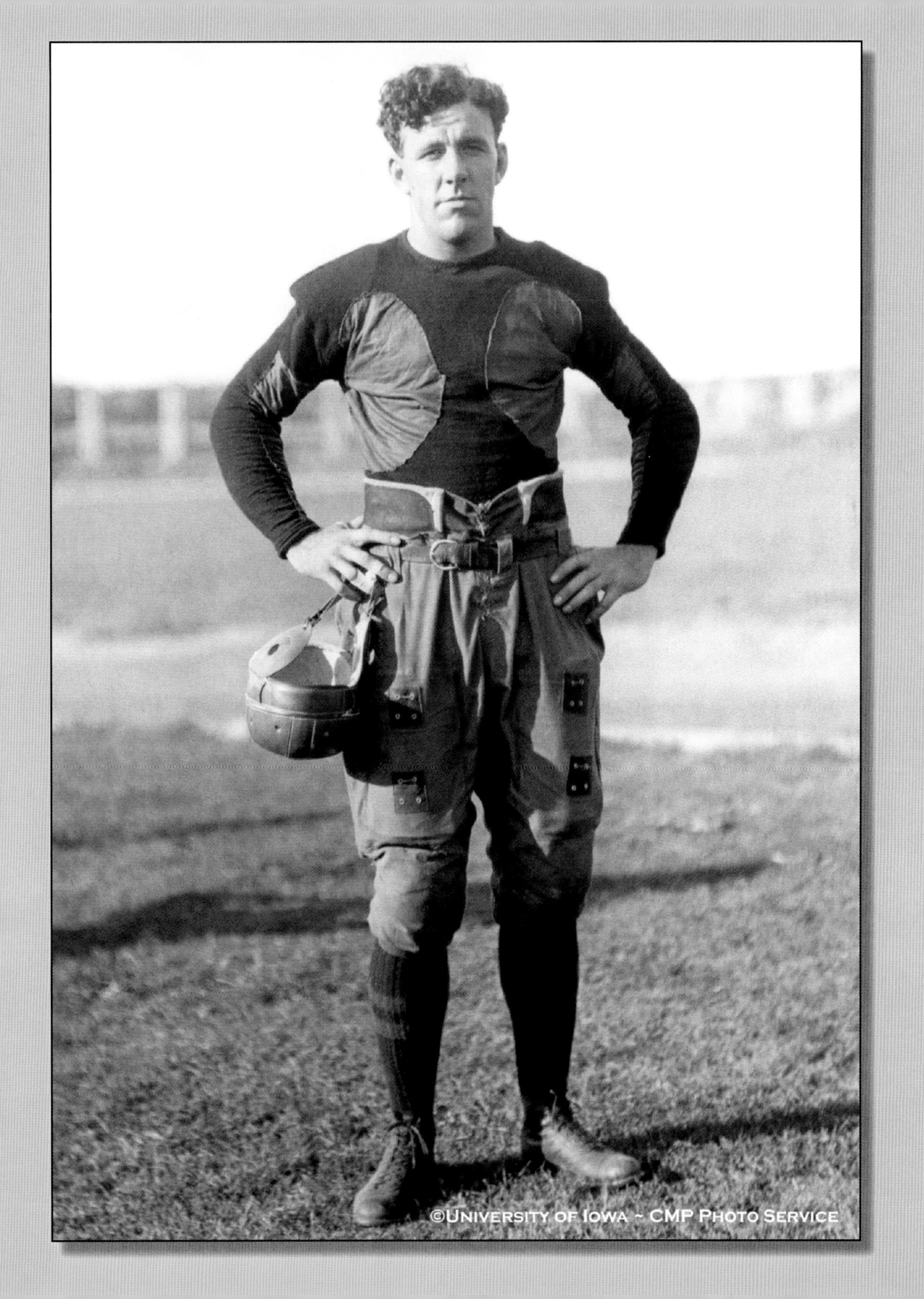
©University of Iowa ~ CMP Photo Service

Calvin Jones

Alex Karras

CALVIN JONES

Lineman

1953–1955

Part of the legendary Steubenville trio from Ohio, Jones turned down a chance to play for Woody Hayes at Ohio State because he wanted to play with his high school teammates, Eddie Vincent and Frank Gilliam.

Ohio State wasn't willing to give all three black players scholarships, whereas Iowa coach Forest Evashevski was. Evashevski obviously knew what he was doing because all three become stars at Iowa and helped lay the foundation for success in the 1950s. Evashevski called Jones "the greatest lineman I ever coached."

Jones was Iowa's first two-time consensus All-American and the school's first winner of the Outland Trophy in 1955. Jones made 22 All-America teams during his career, including a record 16 in 1954.

He also was a three-time All-Big Ten selection and was selected as an offensive lineman on Iowa's all-time team. He was named to the Iowa Lettermen's Club Hall of Fame in 1989.

His jersey No. 62 is one of only two numbers retired in school history, along with Nile Kinnick's.

Jones was establishing himself as a star in the Canadian Football League when he died in an airplane crash on December 9, 1956.

ALEX KARRAS

Lineman

1955–1957

Long before he was Webster's lovable father on television, Karras was an ornery and overpowering lineman at Iowa. He won the Outland Trophy in 1957, just two years after Calvin Jones received the same honor. Karras was also a consensus All-American in 1957. That year, he finished second in the Heisman voting, the highest finish ever for a tackle.

It's no secret that Karras didn't get along with Iowa coach Forest Evashevski. Their feud nearly caused Karras to quit the team, but he persevered to become one of the greatest linemen in the history of college football.

A native of Gary, Indiana, Karras was an all-pro defensive lineman with the Detroit Lions before becoming an actor and author.

RANDY DUNCAN

Quarterback
1956–1958

© University of Iowa – CMP Photo Service

The successor to Rose Bowl–winning quarterback Kenny Ploen, Duncan made quite a name for himself, too, by directing Iowa to a victory in the 1959 Rose Bowl. Duncan won Big Ten and Iowa MVP honors as a senior in 1958 and he finished second in the voting for the Heisman Trophy that same season. He won the Walter Camp Award in 1958 and was named College Player of the Year by three organizations.

Duncan directed the Hawkeyes to a record of 15–2–2 during his two seasons as a starter. In 1958, he led Iowa to the Big Ten championship and a resounding 38–12 win over California in the Rose Bowl. That season, he led the nation in passing yardage (1,397), completion percentage (59.2) and was co-leader in touchdown passes (11). The Des Moines, Iowa, native twice made All-Big Ten and was a consensus All-American as a senior in 1958. He was selected first overall in the 1958 NFL draft, but chose to play in Canada instead.

He went on to become a successful lawyer in Des Moines, where he still lives today. He has also served his community as chairman of the March of Dimes and Cerebral Palsy Campaign, and as president of the YMCA Boys' Home.

	COMP./ATT.	PCT.	YARDS	TDs
Randy Duncan	186/328	.564	2,615	23

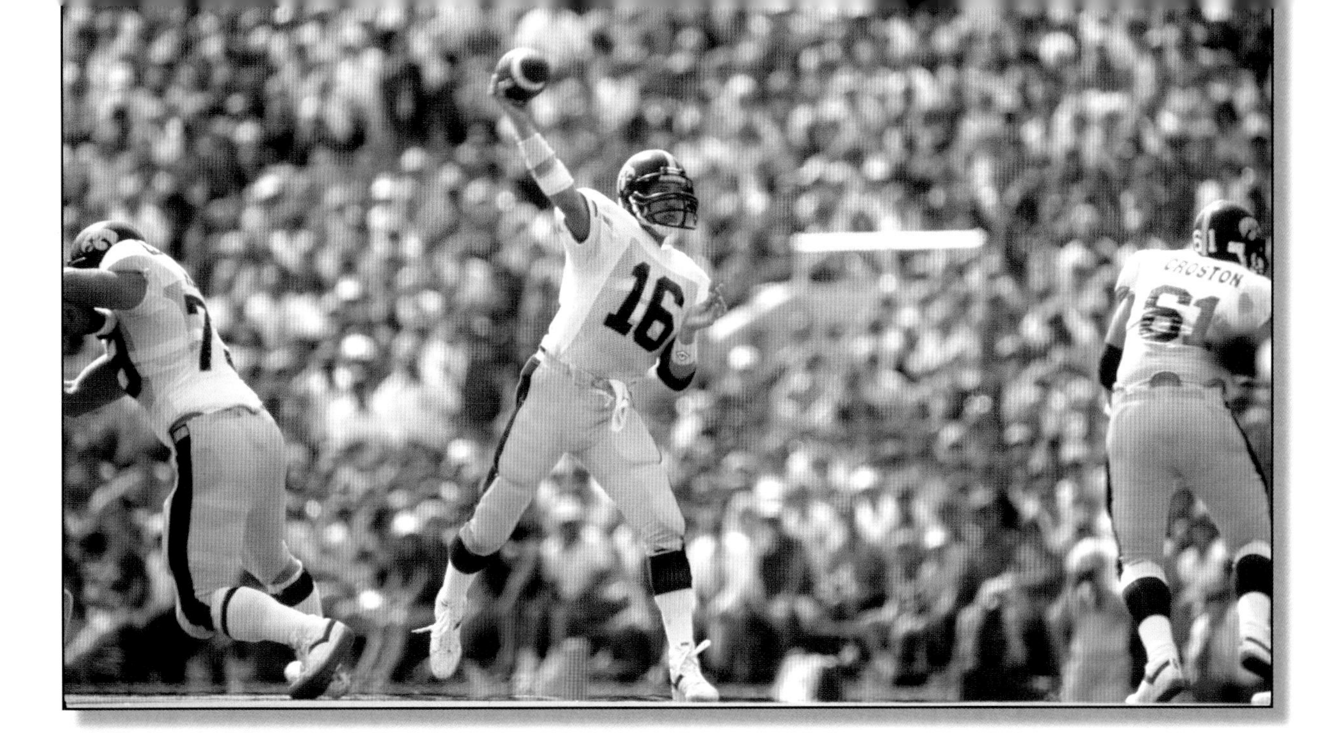

CHUCK LONG

Quarterback
1981–1985

Here's a bit of trivia: Chuck Long is the only player to appear in five bowl games. Long was on the field for two plays in the 1982 Rose Bowl, but since they were his only two plays of the season, they didn't count toward his eligibility. Long then spent four memorable years as Iowa's starting quarterback, a tenure that saw the Hawkeyes make four more bowl trips.

From no-name recruit to Heisman Trophy runner-up, Long's rise as a quarterback is almost too far-fetched to be true. He finished runner-up to Bo Jackson for the 1985 Heisman Trophy in the closest race in the award's history, losing by a mere 45 points.

Long came to Iowa in 1981 as an unheralded option quarterback, but then blossomed into a star pocket passer under Hayden Fry. Long was the first quarterback in Big Ten history to pass for more than 10,000 yards in a career. He also previously held the NCAA record with 22 consecutive completions, which he set against Indiana in 1984, on his way to leading the nation in completion percentage (.661).

He was a three-time All-Big Ten selection and he led Iowa to the Big Ten title and the Rose Bowl in 1985. He also threw a bowl game-record six touchdown passes against Texas in the 1984 Freedom Bowl.

Long was selected by the Detroit Lions in the first round of the 1986 NFL draft and he played nine seasons in the NFL, but never became a star. He returned to Iowa as an assistant coach in the mid-1990s and was hired as the head coach at San Diego State before the 2006 season.

	COMP./ATT.	PCT.	YARDS	TDs
Chuck Long	782/1,203	.650	10,461	74

Iowa fans can point with special pride to the impact that Hawkeyes have had at every position on the football field.

THE QUARTERBACKS

Iowa's quarterback legacy is virtually unmatched in the Big Ten. Not only have the Hawkeyes placed two of their signal callers in the College Football Hall of Fame—Randy Duncan and Chuck Long—but they've also made a recent significant impact on the college football landscape at the game's glamour position.

Al Coupee (1939–1941) was overshadowed by Nile Kinnick during much of his career, but he was never underappreciated by Iowa fans. Coupee played with the toughness and grit that came to symbolize the 1939 Ironmen team. He was a force on defense and a leader on offense. He also is a member of the Iowa Varsity Hall of Fame.

Kenny Ploen (1954–1956) holds a special place in Hawkeye lore; following the 1956 season, he led Iowa to its first victory in the Rose Bowl, in the school's very first appearance in any bowl game. The Clinton, Iowa native was named the Most Valuable Player of that Rose Bowl after leading Iowa to a 35–19 victory over Oregon State. Ploen's 49-yard touchdown run gave Iowa an early lead, and he also completed 9-of-10 passes for 83 yards. He then went on to become a star quarterback in the Canadian Football League.

Gary Snook (1963–1965) led the Hawkeyes in passing for three consecutive seasons and was the first player in school history to pass for more than 2,000 yards in season. He did that as a junior in 1964 with 2,062 passing yards. The combination of Snook to receiver Karl Noonan lit up the Big Ten that season, as Snook was second in the nation in total offense, while Noonan led the nation in receptions. The two hooked up 11 times for 146 yards in Iowa's 28–18 upset of 10th-ranked Washington.

The rise to stardom of **Brad Banks (2001–2002)** was one of the most glorious highlights of Iowa's resurgence under Kirk Ferentz. Banks only needed one season as a starter to be considered among the greatest quarterbacks in school history.

The Belle Glade, Florida, native burst onto the scene as a senior in 2002, going from being a reserve the previous season to the runner-up for the Heisman Trophy.

Kenny Ploen

BRAD BANKS' DREAM SEASON

A few highlights from 2002:

- Completed 170 of 294 passes (57.8 percent) for 2573 yards with 26 touchdowns and 5 interceptions, finishing first in quarterback rating in Division I-A.
- Named AP Player of the Year and was the runner-up for the Heisman Trophy; received the *Chicago Tribune* Silver Football as the MVP of the Big Ten.
- Led the Hawkeyes to an 11–2 record and a tie for the Big Ten crown with Ohio State.

Brad Banks

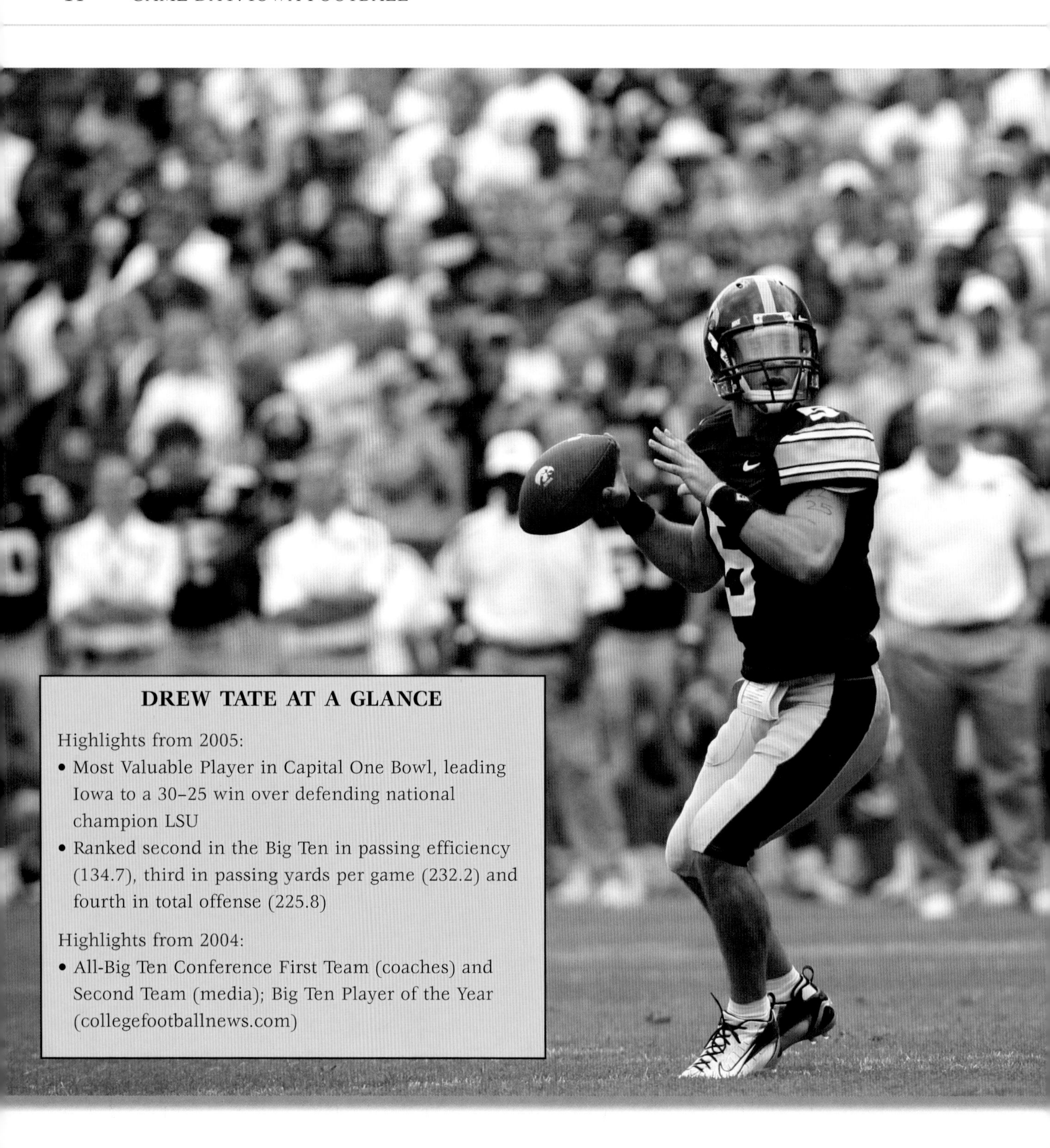

DREW TATE AT A GLANCE

Highlights from 2005:

- Most Valuable Player in Capital One Bowl, leading Iowa to a 30–25 win over defending national champion LSU
- Ranked second in the Big Ten in passing efficiency (134.7), third in passing yards per game (232.2) and fourth in total offense (225.8)

Highlights from 2004:

- All-Big Ten Conference First Team (coaches) and Second Team (media); Big Ten Player of the Year (collegefootballnews.com)

His ability to run and throw caused fits for opposing defenses and made Iowa a force on offense in 2002. He gained 2,996 yards of total offense in 2002 while leading Iowa to a school-record 11 victories.

He also keyed a dramatic come-from-behind victory over Purdue in the fourth quarter by scrambling for a key first down and by throwing a touchdown pass to Dallas Clark in the final minutes.

Banks has played professionally in Canada the past three seasons.

Drew Tate (2003–2006) burst onto the scene by making first-team all-Big Ten as a sophomore in 2004. Tate capped his sophomore season by throwing arguably the greatest touchdown pass in school history—a 56-yard completion to Warren Holloway that defeated LSU on the final play of the 2005 Capital One Bowl. Tate failed to make All-Big Ten after his sophomore season, but he finished his career with impressive statistics. He ranks second in Hawkeye history in completions (665), attempts (1,090), passing yards (8,292), total offense (8,427) and touchdown passes (61).

QUARTERBACKS BY THE NUMBERS

	COMP./ATT.	PCT.	YARDS	TDs
Gary Snook	280/631	.443	3,738	20
Brad Banks	213/362	.588	3,155	30
Drew Tate	665/1,090	.610	8,292	61

THE OFFENSIVE LINEMEN

In typical Big Ten fashion, the Iowa program is known for hard-nosed, intense linemen who clear gaping paths for fleet running backs and protect their quarterbacks from oncoming rushers. When educated fans and NFL scouts talk about the Hawkeyes, the talk invariably turns to the guys in the trenches.

Fred Becker (1915–1916) left Iowa after his sophomore year to fight in World War I. Ten months after enlisting, Becker was killed on July 18, 1918, in France. He left behind a legacy that includes being Iowa's first All-American in football. Becker, a native of Waterloo, Iowa, was an overpowering blocker on the offensive line. Becker was awarded the Belgian War Cross, the *Croix de Guerre*, highest French decoration given for battlefield service, and the American Distinguished Service Cross.

Fred Becker

He was the "Duke" long before John Wayne had the nickname. **Fred "Duke" Slater (1918–1921)** was Iowa's first great lineman, but he was also a trailblazer and a symbol of hope for other black athletes at the time. One of the few blacks to play college football during his time, Slater did nothing to hide it by competing without a helmet. One of the most famous photos in school history shows a helmet-less Slater blocking out four Notre Dame defensive linemen during a victory in 1921.

Slater earned All-America honors in 1921, but his crowning achievement might have occurred in 1946 when 600 sportswriters selected him to the all-time, 11-man Pop Warner squad.

Five years later in 1951, Slater was selected to the National Football Hall of Fame. He went on to become a judge in Chicago and has a dormitory at Iowa named after him.

Fred "Duke" Slater

Iowa coach Ossie Solem called **Francis "Zud" Schammel (1931–1933)** the finest guard he ever coached. Schammel was a consensus All-America pick as a senior, earning first-team honors from both the Associated Press and United Press. He was the first Hawkeye to be honored by both wire services.

Jerry Hilgenberg (1951–1953) was one of the finest guards ever to play for Iowa. Hilgenberg was Forest Evashevski's first All-American at Iowa, earning first-team honors on the Football Writers Association team in 1953. Hilgenberg went on to be an assistant coach at Iowa from 1956 to 1963 and had the opportunity to mentor his younger brother Wally, a Hawkeye standout at the linebacker position.

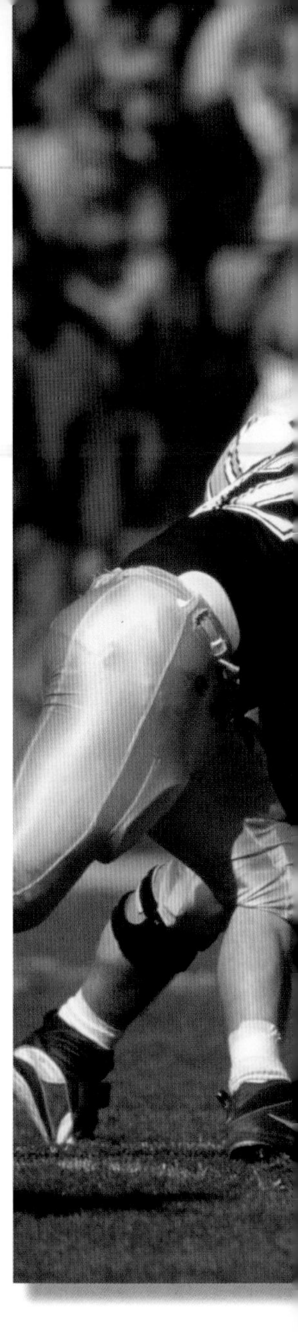

Jerry Hilgenberg

Eric Steinbach

John Niland (1963–1965) made first-team All-America as a senior and was selected fifth overall in the 1966 NFL draft. He went on to have a long and productive career with the Dallas Cowboys.

Sometimes a position switch can make all the difference. Such was the case for **Eric Steinbach (1999–2002)**. His career blossomed after he switched from tight end to offensive guard. He was a consensus All-American as a senior in 2002 and was named the Big Ten Lineman of the Year that season. He was the first player selected in the second round of the 2003 NFL draft by the Cincinnati Bengals. During the 2007 offseason, Steinbach signed a seven-year, $49 million deal with the Cleveland Browns.

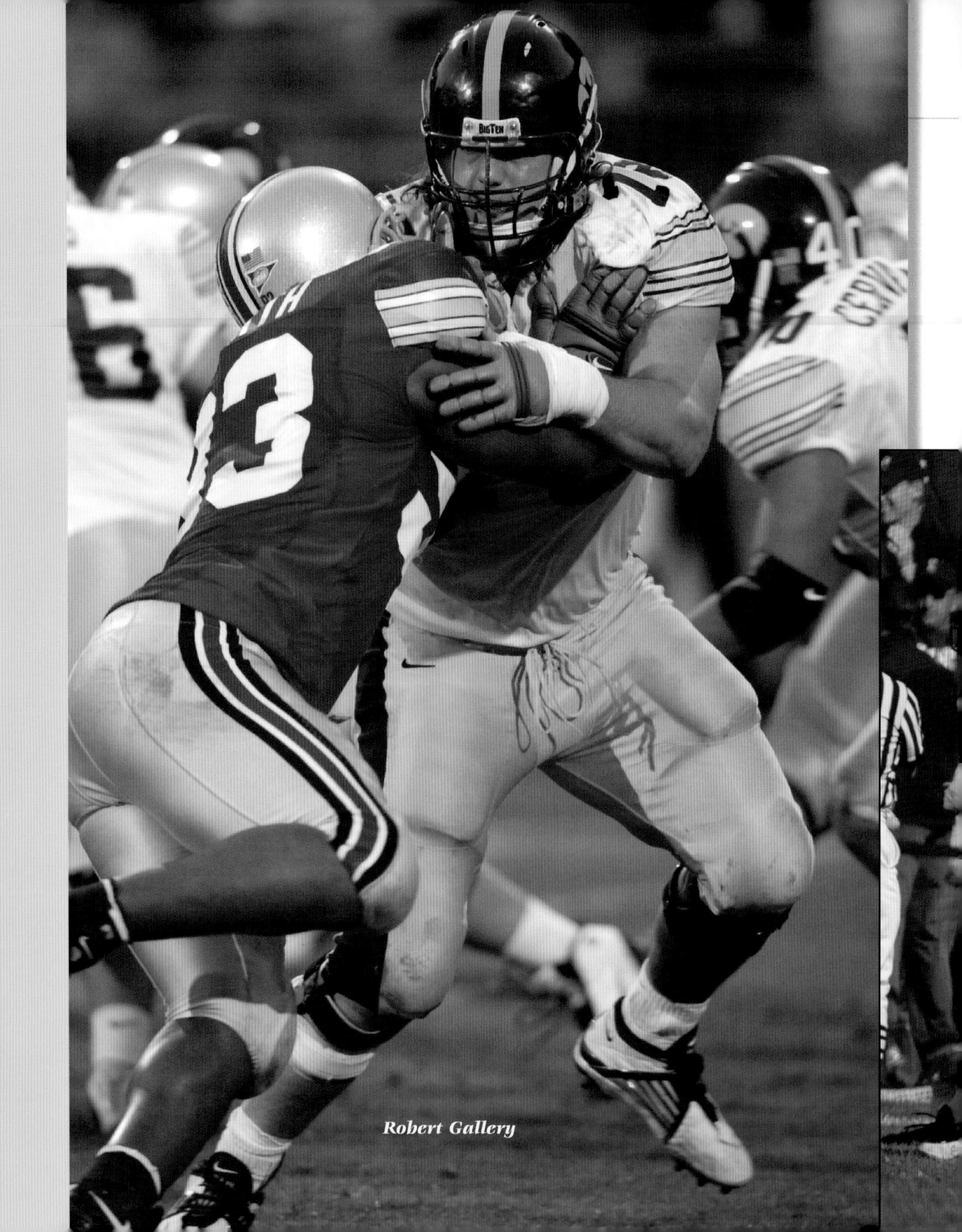

Robert Gallery

The great **Robert Gallery (2000–2003)** followed Steinbach's lead by switching from tight end then becoming an All-America offensive lineman. Gallery started at left tackle for Iowa for three seasons and won the Outland Trophy as a senior in 2003. His size and athleticism separated him from most college offensive linemen.

He was selected second overall in the 2004 NFL draft by the Oakland Raiders and signed a contract worth about $60 million.

A former junior-college transfer, **Marshal Yanda (2005–2006)** accomplished a lot in only two seasons at Iowa. He started both seasons and made first-team All-Big Ten as a senior in 2006. Coach Kirk Ferentz called Yanda one of the best offensive linemen he has ever coached, which is quite a testimony considering Ferentz's background and his ability to judge offensive line talent.

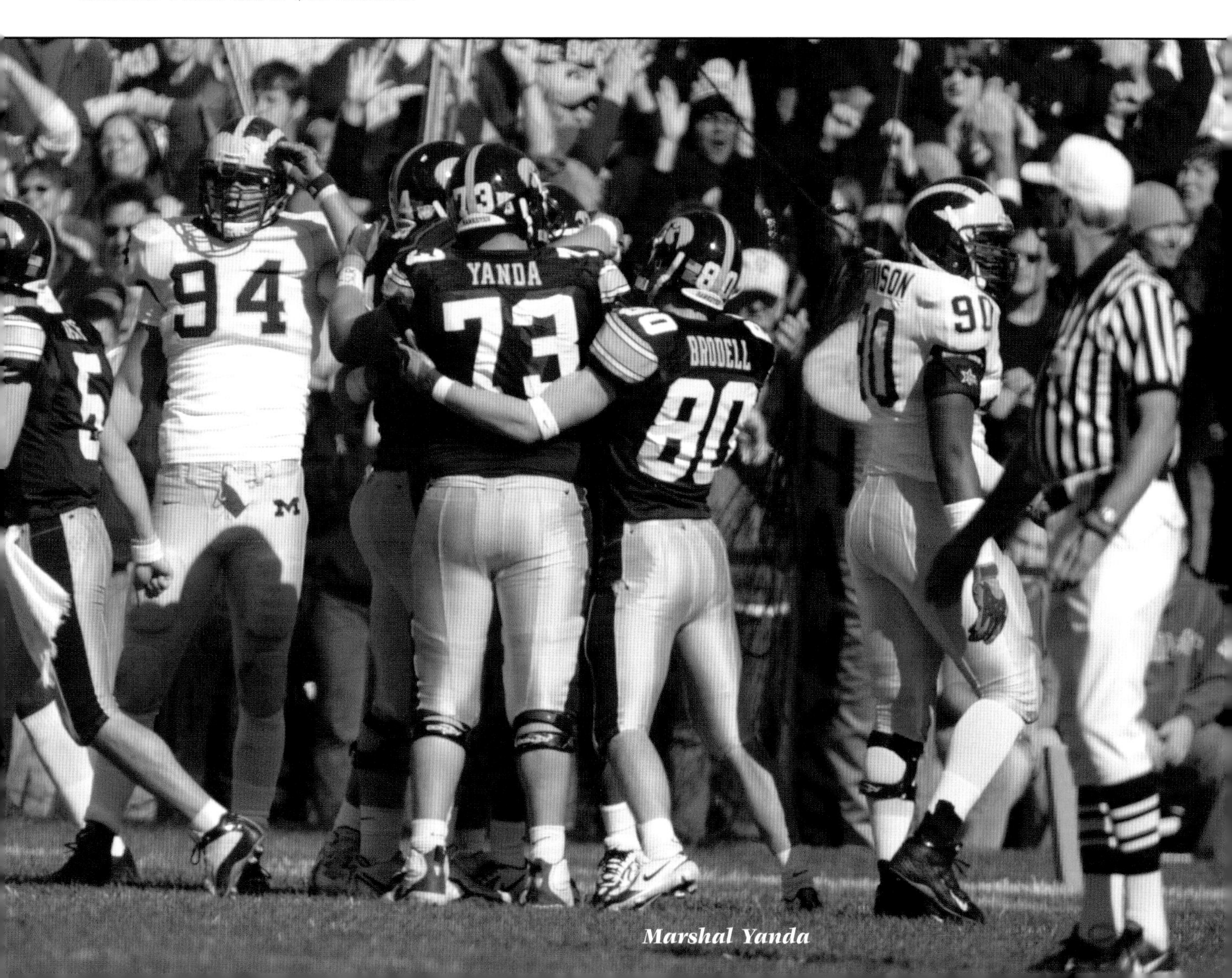

Marshal Yanda

The Skill Players

Iowa's skill player tradition is virtually unmatched. While nine Hawkeye quarterbacks have been All-Big Ten since 1983 alone, those quarterbacks have had plenty of help in the form of sure-handed receivers and explosive runners.

Let's start with the great running backs of Hawkeye history.

RUNNING BACKS

Carleton Holbrok (1895–1896) has the distinction of being the first black player in the history of the Iowa program, but he did more than just break the color barrier. Holbrok led the Hawkeyes with 12 touchdowns in 1896, which would be considered a lot today but was a startling figure back then.

Halfback **Willis Glassgow (1927–1929)** became the first Iowan to win the Silver Football Award, given annually to the Most Valuable Player in the Big Ten. He earned that distinction as a senior in 1929. He also made Grantland Rice's first-team All-America squad in 1929.

Willis Glassgow

Halfback/defensive back **Joe Laws (1931–1933)** was the beneficiary of Zud Schammel's blocking on the offensive side of the ball, but he did much on his own, too. Laws was the second player from Iowa to be named Most Valuable Player in the Big Ten in 1933 and just the ninth overall. He led Iowa in scoring in conference games that season while guiding the team to a 5–3 record.

Dick Crayne (1932–1934) led Iowa in rushing in 1933 and 1934 with 655 and 432 yards, respectively. He also scored seven touchdowns in both seasons.

Ozzie Simmons (1934–1936) was one of the most exciting players in the school's history, but that only tells part of his legacy.

Simmons was a black man playing a white man's game in the mid-1930s, and he paid a heavy price for being a trailblazer. He was abused physically on the field and verbally off it.

Ozzie Simmons

Joe Laws

Emlen Tunnell

Bill Reichardt

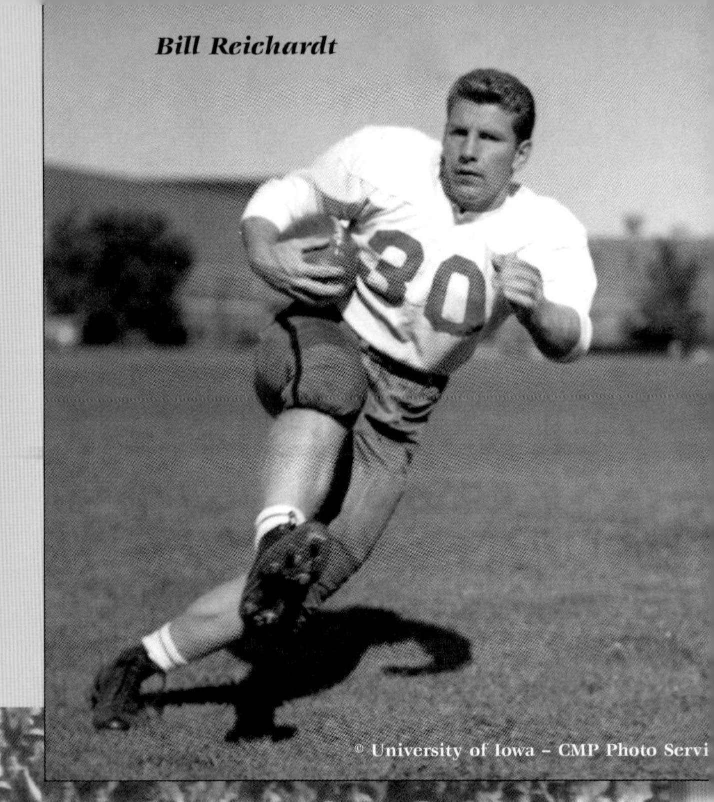

Eddie Vincent (No. 41)

In fact, Floyd of Rosedale, the traveling pig statue that goes to the winner of the Iowa-Minnesota game, was created because Hawkeye fans were upset with how Simmons was treated by the Minnesota players. In order to ease tensions between the two schools, the governors from both states made a friendly wager in 1935, with the winning team getting possession of the pig statue until the next game.

Simmons grew up in Fort Worth, Texas and matriculated to Iowa after learning about Duke Slater's success at the school.

Simmons electrified fans with his speed and elusive running style. He rushed for more than 1,500 yards as a Hawkeye and had eight touchdown runs of more than 50 yards. He also was a star defensive back at Iowa and twice earned second-team All-America honors.

Simmons wanted to play professional football, but the NFL had an unwritten rule at the time that prohibited players of color. Simmons went on to become an elementary school teacher in Chicago, where he died on September 26, 2001.

He became a charter member of the Iowa Varsity Club Hall of Fame in 1989.

Quarterback/halfback **Emlen Tunnell (1946–1947)** earned more lasting fame as a professional, but he left his mark in Iowa City as well. Tunnell showed his versatility by leading Iowa in passing in 1946 and in receiving the next season. Tunnell went on to become an All-Pro defensive back in the National Football League, keying the great Giant defenses of the 1950s. He was also the first black player inducted into the Pro Football Hall of Fame and the first black assistant coach in the NFL.

The greatest tribute that fullback **Bill Reichardt (1949–1951)** earned was being named Big Ten MVP for a team that didn't win a single conference game in 1951. Reichardt rushed for more than 150 yards against both Michigan and Minnesota in 1951, and he finished with 737 rushing yards overall that season. The Iowa City, Iowa, native finished his career with 1,665 rushing yards, which at the time had been exceeded by only Aubrey Devine and Gordon Locke among Hawkeye backs. Reichardt also made 51-of-63 PAT kicks during his career. He entered the clothing business after college and owned a very successful clothing store in Des Moines for years.

Of the Steubenville trio, halfback **Eddie Vincent (1953–1955)** supplied the speed. He still holds the school record for the longest run from scrimmage—a 96-yard touchdown dash against Purdue in 1954. He led Iowa in rushing as a junior and senior, and he made All-Big Ten and various all-Midwest teams during his career. He entered politics after leaving Iowa and became mayor of Inglewood, California.

Silas McKinnie (1965–1967) led the Hawkeyes in rushing for three consecutive seasons from 1965 to 1967. His nine rushing touchdowns in 1967 set a school record at the time.

Ed Podolak (1966–1968) never played on a winning team at Iowa, but it was through no fault of his own. He started his career at quarterback, then switched to running back, and was effective at both positions. His 286-yard rushing performance against Northwestern in 1968 stood as the school single-game rushing mark for nearly 30 years. He finished his career with 1,710 rushing yards and 4,026 total yards. He later became a star running back for the Kansas City Chiefs and has since done color commentary for Iowa football games for the past 20 years. He also owns a resort in Costa Rico and lives in Vail, Colo.

Jon Lazar (1975–1978), a hard-charging fullback from Tama, Iowa, led the Hawkeyes in rushing as a sophomore, junior and senior.

Dennis Mosley (1976–1979) was Coach Hayden Fry's first star running back at Iowa. Mosley led the Hawkeyes in rushing in Fry's debut season in 1979 with 1,267 yards and 12 touchdowns.

Dennis Mosley

Silas McKinnie

Ed Podolak

Chicago native **Eddie Phillips (1980–1983)** was another one of Hayden Fry's early star recruits at Iowa. Phillips helped lay the foundation for future success by rushing for 2,177 yards and scoring 19 touchdowns.

You name it and **Ronnie Harmon (1982–1985)** did it for the Hawkeyes. He played receiver during his first two seasons and showed tremendous potential before switching to running back for his last two seasons. Harmon is Iowa's all-time leader in all-purpose yards (4,978), and his 2,045 receiving yards and 2,271 rushing yards rank third and seventh in school history, respectively. Harmon's career ended in controversy, though, when he fumbled four times during the 1986 Rose Bowl. He also was accused of taking money from a sports agent, but he still played for a decade in the NFL, where he distinguished himself as a quality third-down back.

Eddie Phillips

Ronnie Harmon

How good was **Sedrick Shaw (1993–1996)** at Iowa? Good enough to keep Tavian Banks on the bench for three seasons and good enough to be Iowa's all-time leading rusher. Shaw used speed, quickness and durability to top the Hawkeye rushing charts with 4,156 career yards. He rushed for more than 1,000 yards in three of his four seasons at Iowa, including a personal-best 1,477 yards as a junior in 1995.

His highest single-game rushing output was 250 yards on 42 carries during a victory at Michigan State in 1995.

A native of Austin, Texas, Shaw played briefly with the New England Patriots, Cincinnati Bengals and Cleveland Browns after leaving Iowa.

Sedrick Shaw

Tavian Banks

Tavian Banks (1994–1997) was slowed by injuries and by the presence of Shaw while at Iowa, but he is still the school's third all-time leading rusher with 2,977 yards.

He gained more than half of those yards during his record-breaking senior season in 1997. Banks set the Iowa single-season rushing record with 1,691 yards and the single-game rushing record with 314 yards against Tulsa in 1997. His elusive running style distinguished him from most Iowa running backs, many of whom relied on power.

Banks's NFL career was cut short by a devastating knee injury.

Ladell Betts

Ladell Betts (1998–2001) played on some bad teams at Iowa, including the 1999 squad that finished 1–10, but he still ran hard and compiled some gaudy statistics. He also took a pounding, but rarely got injured. He is Iowa's second-leading rusher of all time with 3,686 yards.

Betts currently plays for the Washington Redskins and just recorded his first career 1,000-yard rushing season in 2006.

Fred Russell (2001–2003) was small in size (5'8") but large in terms of production. The Inkster, Michigan, native led Iowa in rushing in both the 2002 and 2003 seasons with 1,264 and 1,355 yards, respectively. He also was named the most valuable player at the 2004 Outback Bowl after rushing for 150 yards on 21 carries.

RUNNING BACKS BY THE NUMBERS

	ATT.	YARDS	AVG.	TDs
Bill Reichardt	384	1,665	4.3	6
Silas McKinnie	254	1,390	5.5	9
Ed Podolak	407	1,710	4.2	14
Jon Lazar	304	1,225	4.0	7
Dennis Mosley	458	2,113	4.6	14
Eddie Phillips	465	2,177	4.7	19
Ronnie Harmon	443	2,271	5.1	22
Sedrick Shaw	837	4,156	5.0	33
Tavian Banks	505	2,977	5.9	33
Ladell Betts	831	3,686	4.4	25
Fred Russell	514	2,760	5.4	17

Fred Russell

ENDS AND RECEIVERS

End **Lester Belding (1919–1921)** was Iowa's first consensus All-American, earning that distinction as a sophomore in 1919. He was a three-time All-Big Ten selection and considered one of the greatest pass catchers of his era. The Mason City, Iowa, native also starred in track at Iowa.

Erwin Prasse (1937–1939) was voted team captain as a senior over Nile Kinnick, which says a little something about Prasse's reputation among his teammates. He was a unanimous All-Big Ten selection in 1939 and was a member of the United Press All-America second team.

The good hands component of the famed Steubenville trio, **Frank Gilliam (1953–1956)** led Iowa in receiving in both 1953 and 1954. He also was a key member of Iowa's 1956 team that was victorious in the Rose Bowl. He went on to become a scout in the NFL and currently works for the Minnesota Vikings as Vice President of Player Personnel.

Jim Gibbons (1955–1957) earned a special place in Iowa lore. Many rank his 16-yard touchdown catch that defeated Ohio State 6–0 in 1956 and earned Iowa its first trip to the Rose Bowl as the greatest moment in school history. Gibbons led Iowa in receiving as a sophomore, junior and senior. He also earned All-Big Ten honors twice and made various All-America teams as a senior.

Curt Merz (1957–1959) was acknowledged by many as the finest end to play under Coach Forest Evashevski at Iowa. He earned first-team All-America honors by the Football Writers Association and *Look* magazine in 1958.

Sometimes, a key recruit can get the ball rolling for a school at a certain position. Such

Lester Belding

Erwin Prasse

was the case for **Keith Chappelle (1979–1980)**. The former junior college transfer from California helped lay the foundation for success under Hayden Fry by becoming one of the top receivers in the Big Ten. Chappelle only played two seasons at Iowa, but he made the most of them. He was the first player in school history to surpass the 1,000-yard receiving mark. He caught 64 passes for 1,037 yards and six touchdowns as a senior in 1980.

Dave Moritz (1980–1983) was a big-play machine for the Hawkeyes. His career average of 17.5 yards per catch ranks among the highest in school history. He also ranks fifth in school history with 1,912 receiving yards on 109 catches.

Frank Gilliam

Jim Gibbons

Tim Dwight

> *"Still to this day, when they come out of the tunnel, when I see the swarm, it still gets to me, brings tears of emotion."*
>
> —MARV COOK

Speaking of big plays, when you think of big-play Hawkeye receivers, you think of **Quinn Early (1984–1987).** He is still one of only three Iowa players to finish with more than 1,000 yards receiving in a season. He accomplished that in 1987 with 63 catches for 1,004 yards and 10 touchdowns. He enjoyed a long and productive career in the NFL after leaving Iowa.

Iowa has built a reputation as something of a Tight End U. That tradition really started in earnest with **Marv Cook (1985–1988)**.

Not only is Cook one of the greatest tight ends in school history, but he also made one the greatest catches in school history.

Cook was a consensus All-American in 1988 and was named to Iowa's all-time team. He is Iowa's all-time leading receiver among tight ends with 126 catches and ranks seventh overall. His 28-yard touchdown catch with six seconds remaining carried Iowa past Ohio State in a 29–27 thriller in Columbus in 1987.

Cook led the Big Ten in catches as a senior in 1988, and he twice was named All-Pro in the NFL as a member of the New England Patriots. He grew up in tiny West Branch, Iowa, which is about 10 miles east of the Iowa campus and the hometown of former President Herbert Hoover.

Former Iowa coach Hayden Fry referred to receiver/return specialist **Tim Dwight (1994–1997)** as the greatest competitor he ever coached—and that covers a lot of players.

Dwight grew up in Iowa City and was a local legend before he ever became a Hawkeye. He was a consensus All-America return specialist and finished seventh in the voting for the 1997 Heisman Trophy.

Dwight led the nation with a 16.7 punt-return average as a senior in 1997, and he set an Iowa and Big Ten record for career punt return yardage (1,102). He also set a Big Ten record by returning five punts for touchdowns during his career, including three in 1997. Dwight is believed to be the only player in college football history to return punts for touchdowns against Michigan, Ohio State and Penn State.

But wait—there's more. Dwight is also Iowa's all-time leading receiver with 2,271 yards despite only being about 5'9" and weighing 185 pounds.

He is a nine-year NFL veteran and currently plays for the New York Jets.

Dallas Clark

Kevin Kasper (1997–2000) came to Iowa as a walk-on and left as one of the top receivers in school history. He played on some bad teams at Iowa, but still finished his career with 157 catches for 1,974 yards and 11 touchdowns.

Tight end **Dallas Clark (1999–2002)** is another Hawkeye who has found fame at the professional level, but his impact in Iowa City was undeniable. Clark's rise to stardom in 2002 was as unexpected as his team's rise to national power that season. Clark came to Iowa as a walk-on linebacker, but he left as a junior in 2002 as the winner of the John Mackey Award, which goes to the nation's best tight end.

He helped Iowa finish undefeated in the Big Ten for the first time in 80 years in 2002 while earning consensus All-America honors. He finished his career with 81 catches for 1,281 yards in just two seasons as a tight end.

Clark was selected in the first round of the 2003 NFL draft by the Indianapolis Colts and now is one of Peyton Manning's favorite targets.

Ed Hinkel (2002–2005) wasn't flashy or explosive, but he probably had the best hands of any receiver to play for Kirk Ferentz at Iowa. The Erie, Pennsylvania, native finished his career with 1,588 receiving yards and 15 touchdowns. Like Tim Dwight, he also excelled as a punt returner.

RECEIVERS BY THE NUMBERS

	REC.	YARDS	AVG.	TDs
Jim Gibbons	69	1,099	15.9	11
Keith Chappelle	86	1,377	16.0	9
Dave Moritz	109	1,912	17.5	9
Ronnie Harmon	146	2,045	14.0	10
Quinn Early	106	1,845	17.4	13
Marv Cook	126	1,825	14.5	6
Tim Dwight	139	2,271	16.3	21
Kevin Kasper	157	1,974	12.6	11
Dallas Clark	81	1,281	15.8	8
Ed Hinkel	135	1,588	11.8	15

Defensive Players

Iowa has always played a style of defense that features both skill and tenacity. These defenders lead the list of Hawkeye greats.

DEFENSIVE LINEMEN

Defensive tackle **John Harty (1977–1980)** was a key member of Iowa's 1981 defense that dominated opponents and carried the Hawkeyes to the Rose Bowl. He earned first-team All-Big Ten honors and some All-America recognition before moving on to the NFL, where he played for the San Francisco 49ers.

Before he was star in the NFL, defensive end **Andre Tippett (1980–1981)** terrorized quarterbacks in the Big Ten. He grew up in Newark, N.J., and only played two seasons at Iowa, but that was enough time for Tippett to become one of the greatest defensive players in school history.

He was the defensive star for Iowa's 1981 Rose Bowl team under Coach Hayden Fry. He also was Fry's first consensus All-American at Iowa and a defensive end on Iowa's all-time team.

Tippett's monster 1980 season included 20 tackles for 153 yards in losses (still a season record for lost yardage). He also led the Big Ten in tackles for losses that season.

Tippett had a long and successful career with the New England Patriots after leaving Iowa.

Leroy Smith (1988–1991) came to Iowa as a running back and left as a consensus All-America defensive end in 1991. Smith lived in the opponent's backfield in 1991, when he set a Big Ten record with 18 quarterback sacks. He also set a school record with five sacks during a 16–9 victory at Ohio State in 1991.

A native of Sicklerville, New Jersey, Smith helped Iowa finish 10–1–1 as a senior in 1991. He was named the Big Ten Defensive Player of the Year that season.

Jared DeVries (1995–1998) was a consensus All-American as a senior in 1998 and now plays for the Detroit Lions. Intense and unstoppable, DeVries holds Iowa records for tackles for losses in a career (78) and sacks (42). He started for four years and recorded 260 tackles. He also earned MVP honors at the 1995 Sun Bowl and the 1996 Alamo Bowl.

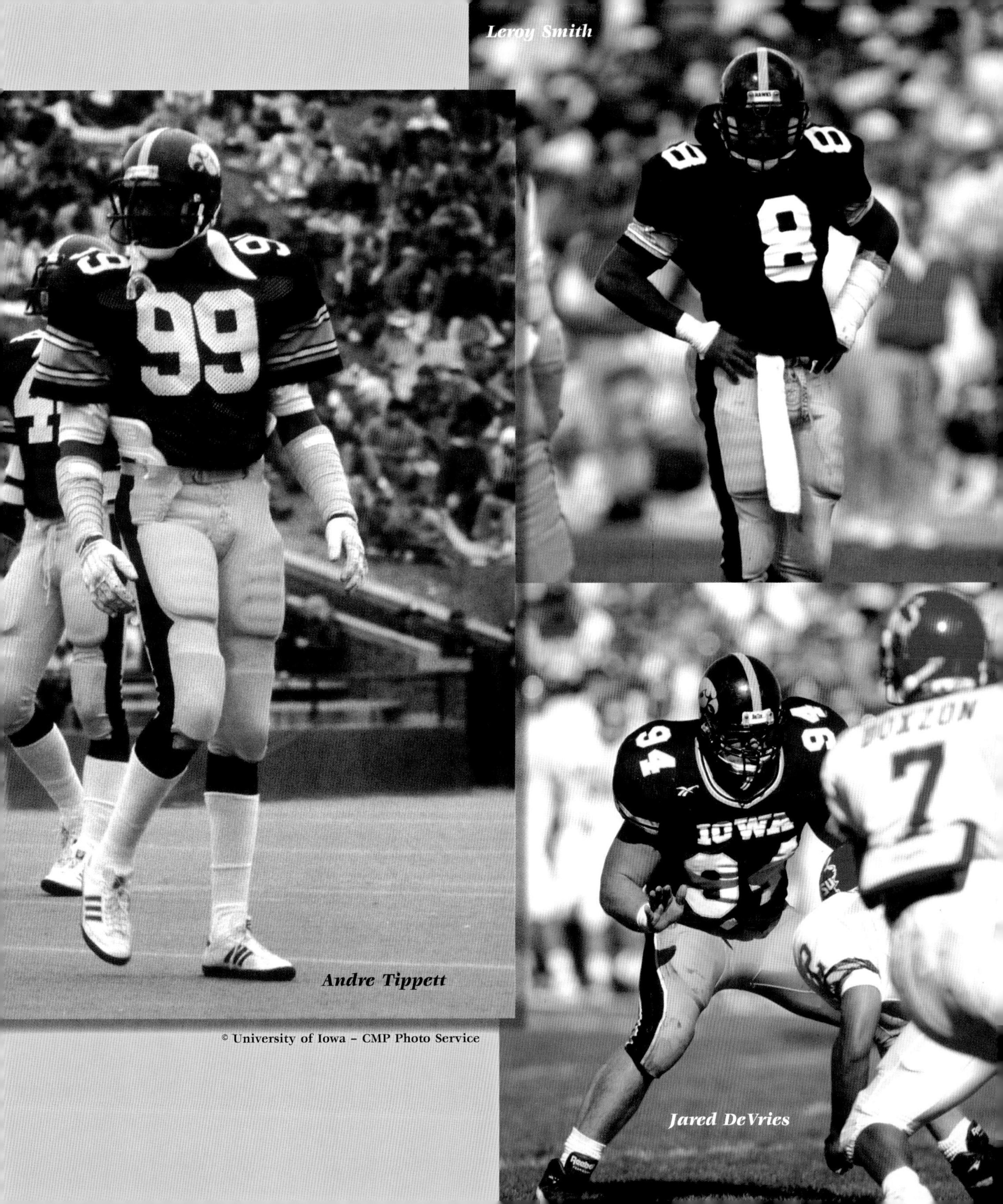

Leroy Smith

Andre Tippett

Jared DeVries

Abdul Hodge

Larry Station

LINEBACKERS

Nebraska's rare loss of an in-state recruit turned into Iowa's gain in a huge way. **Larry Station (1982–1985)** is one is of only two Hawkeyes to earn consensus All-America honors twice and the only player in school history to lead the team in tackles four times.

A native of Omaha, Nebraska, Station earned All-America mention all four years at Iowa and made All-Big Ten three times. He started the last 42 games in his career and was a finalist for the Lombardi and Butkus awards in 1985.

Abdul Hodge (2002–2005) and **Chad Greenway (2002–2005)** formed what many consider to be the greatest linebacker combination in school history.

Hodge started for three seasons and twice made first-team All-Big Ten. He now plays for the Green Bay Packers after being selected in the third round of the 2006 NFL draft.

Hodge, who was born in the Virgin Islands, ranks third in school history with 453 tackles.

Greenway grew up on a farm in South Dakota and was ignored by virtually all the major programs in the country. But the Iowa coaches saw something special in him. They saw a big, fast and versatile athlete with a great motor and work ethic. Greenway played quarterback and defensive back in high school before growing into a linebacker at Iowa. He had a knack for making the big play and is ranked fifth in school history with 416 tackles. The Minnesota Vikings selected Greenway in the first round of the 2006 draft, but he missed the entire season because of a knee injury.

Chad Greenway

The following article appeared in the 2005 edition of Athlon Sports' Big Ten preseason college football annual.

ONE-TWO PUNCH

Hawkeye Headliners May Be Nation's Best Tandem

One grew up in South Florida, wears dreadlocks and speaks softly. The other grew up on a farm in South Dakota and speaks whenever he feels like it.

Iowa linebackers Abdul Hodge and Chad Greenway are polar opposites — until they take the football field. Then they become two of the best defensive players in the country, a devastating one-two punch that combined for 229 tackles last season. Both players also made first-team All-Big Ten in 2004 and now rank among the premier linebackers in the country.

"Even though we came from different backgrounds we share the same characteristics," Hodge says. "We're both hard workers. We're both tough. And we want to win."

Iowa fans can't mention one without the other, almost like they're joined at the hip. Fans also can't seem to agree on who is better. But there is no debate over their popularity or how valuable they are to the Iowa program, which is coming off three consecutive top-10 finishes in both wire service polls.

"We're not roommates, but we might as well be off the field," Greenway says. "We have classes together. You can always see us around campus doing stuff together. We're obviously very different in a lot of ways, but we're very similar in the way we play football and how we compete. And I think that's what makes us good friends."

Hodge feels the same way about their friendship. He says being close off the field makes them better players on the field.

"We've very close," Hodge says. "We know each other's family and stuff. So we've got a good feel for each other and that carries out on to the field."

The extent of their friendship became apparent after Greenway learned that he was named to *Playboy* magazine's preseason All-America team. While he was thrilled with being selected, it's who didn't get picked that bothered Greenway.

Chad Greenway

Abdul Hodge

"It's kind of tough when people like Abdul don't make it when they're as good or better than I am," Greenway says. "It's tough to get an honor like that, but it's exciting at the same time."

Iowa coach Kirk Ferentz admires the bond between his two star linebackers. Ferentz says he knew that Hodge's *Playboy* snub would hurt Greenway.

"I'm not surprised by Chad's response," Ferentz says. "If Abdul had been the guy selected, it would have been the same thing in reverse. They both think the same way."

They also don't mind sharing the spotlight. In fact, Greenway says he prefers it that way.

"I think we kind of take the light off of each other," he says. "It's easier to share than to have it by yourself."

Greenway seems unfazed by his success or the hype surrounding the Iowa program. He was raised to be humble and says that never will change.

"Hopefully, by now I'm mature enough to handle it," Greenway says. "My parents will slap me if I'm not. I think it just goes back to knowing where you came from. If I got too big of a head, my parents would let me know."

Greenway comes from tiny Mount Vernon, S.D., which has very little in common with Hodge's hometown of Fort Lauderdale, Fla. Greenway grew up on a 1,500-acre farm; Hodge grew up in one of the more densely populated areas in the country.

"It's kind of cool the relationships you get from college and the college football experience," Greenway says. "It's fun seeing how everything meshes together and works out.

"It would be interesting to see (Abdul) go up there and see how everything works on the farm and see him around the animals and stuff."

Greenway was ignored by virtually all of the major programs in the nation primary because he played nine-man football at Mt. Vernon High School. South Dakota is considered a wasteland when it comes to producing Division I-A football recruits. Nebraska dips in every now and then to sign a player, but for the most part, South Dakota is off the recruiting radar.

Nevertheless, Iowa defensive coordinator Norm Parker saw something special in Greenway. Parker saw a big-boned kid with size, speed and toughness making plays all over the field as a quarterback and defensive back. He saw a kid with a good attitude and a good work ethic that came from working long hours on the farm.

"A lot of people don't even call that football," Greenway says of the nine-man game. "Well, I certainly think it's football. As Coach Parker has always said to me, football players come from everywhere. It doesn't matter what you played or where you played."

Iowa recruited Greenway as an athlete then allowed him to pick his position. He grew into a linebacker, but never has outgrown his athleticism.

Hodge, meanwhile, had more options than Greenway coming out of high school. He could have signed with Auburn or North Carolina State, but he liked what was happening at Iowa.

"I felt comfortable around the players and coaches," Hodge says. "They were on the verge of turning the program around, and I wanted to be a part of that."

While it is not unusual for a kid from talent-rich South Florida to become a college football star, Greenway's path to stardom is unusual. Greenway appreciates his success, but he isn't overwhelmed by it.

"It's not really surreal, it's probably just a better story," Greenway says. "It gives people something to write about, the fact that I didn't come from a good 11-man school. I come from the prairie in South Dakota. It's just different and people like that."

Hodge and Greenway are different when it comes to playing linebacker. Hodge, a 6'2", 234-pounder, is a classic run stopper, a big hit waiting to happen between the tackles. He is the guy in the middle of those short-yardage situations, where helmets and shoulder pads crash together.

Greenway, on the other hand, is more versatile and more likely to make a big play from anywhere on the field. He can leap to make an interception as easily as he can wrap his arms to make a tackle.

He intercepted three passes last season, returning one for a touchdown.

It's that kind of versatility that caused NFL draft guru Mel Kiper Jr. to say that Greenway would have been among the top linebackers selected in the 2005 draft had he chosen to come out.

Rumors and speculation had Greenway and Hodge both seriously contemplating leaving school early to enter the '05 draft. However, they both set the record straight during spring practice.

"It's funny because people think they know, but they don't," Greenway says. "It never crossed either of our minds, I don't think, to go and to really even think about it because we knew we had a lot of work to do."

"I didn't consider it at all, it was just a quick thought," says Hodge, who stayed in college despite having a baby daughter. "I wanted to come back and finish school. I could have finished school in May, but we've got a lot of stuff to accomplish out here. I just wanted to come back and give the university another year."

Greenway says he wasn't ready to play in the NFL or ready to leave college after his junior season. He's simply having too much fun being a Hawkeye.

"I didn't feel like I was even close to being able to take that step," Greenway says. "I feel like there's way too much for me to learn and to do yet on the football field.

"And I could never have left my friends here. I think we have too much going for us."

Greenway has thrived as an underdog since coming to Iowa. He found motivation last season from a magazine that picked him as the most overrated player in the Big Ten.

"I take that stuff to heart and I love to play with stuff like that within my bag, like the overrated thing," Greenway says. "I'm sure somebody will write something. I'm waiting."

He isn't sure where the time has gone, however.

"It's unreal how fast it's gone, the last four years," Greenway says. "It's just unbelievable where I came from to where I am now."

DEFENSIVE BACKS

Craig Clemons (1969–1971) stood out for some bad teams at Iowa. He led the Hawkeyes in interceptions as both a junior and senior. He also had a long career in the NFL with the Chicago Bears.

Ohio native **Bob Stoops (1979–1982)** was a member of Bob Commings' last recruiting class at Iowa in 1978, but Stoops became a star under Hayden Fry. Stoops played safety for the Hawkeyes and was known for his vicious hits. He made first-team All-Big Ten as a senior in 1982 and was key player for Iowa's 1981 Rose Bowl team. Stoops is now the head coach at Oklahoma, where he led the Sooners to a national title in 2000.

Craig Clemons
©UNIVERSITY OF IOWA ~ CMP PHOTO SERVICE

Bob's younger brother **Mike Stoops (1981–1984)** had many of the same attributes on the field as Bob did. Mike was also a very physical defensive back who made first-team All-Big Ten in both his junior and senior seasons. He also entered the coaching profession and has brought his particular brand of intensity to Tucson as the head coach at Arizona.

Damien Robinson (1993–1996) played safety with the same nasty attitude that Bob Sanders later brought to the position. Robinson was considered one of the hardest hitters in the Big Ten as a senior in 1996. He also made first-team All-Big Ten as a senior then went on to enjoy a long and productive career in the NFL.

Mike Stoops

Bob Sanders

Bob Sanders (2000–2003) came to Iowa with only two scholarship offers, but he left as arguably the greatest defensive back in school history. He now plays for the Indianapolis Colts and has become one of the best defensive backs and hardest hitters in the NFL. He also boasts a Super Bowl ring courtesy of the Colts' defensive domination during the 2007 postseason.

Sanders was a four-year starter at Iowa and a fan favorite because of his physical playing style at strong safety. He made first-team All-Big Ten three times and was a terror on special teams.

Iowa decided to offer Sanders a scholarship on the advice of his high school coach in Erie, Pennsylvania, the late Joe Moore. Moore also was Kirk Ferentz's coach in high school, and the two had become close friends.

Quarterbacks had to be aware of **Jovon Johnson (2002–2005)** at all times or he would make them pay. He finished his career with 17 interceptions, which is the second-highest total in school history behind Nile Kinnick's and Devon Mitchell's 18 interceptions. Johnson also returned punts for the Hawkeyes.

SPECIALISTS

The kicking game at Iowa has borne a special stamp of excellence over the years. Two specialists in particular deserve mention here.

Rarely do fans get excited to watch a punter, but that was the case with **Reggie Roby (1979–1982)** at Iowa. Fans were amazed at the distance and hang time on Roby's punts.

The Waterloo, Iowa, native was without question the greatest punter in school history and one of the greatest in the history of college football.

He was a consensus All-American as a junior in 1981 after breaking a 32-year old NCAA record for punting average with a 49.8 average. He also holds the national career punting average record and twice led the nation in punting during his career.

Roby twice made first-team All-Big Ten and punted for nearly four-and-a-half miles as a collegian. He earned All-Pro honors in the NFL and played with Miami, Washington and Tampa Bay.

Tragically, Roby died suddenly in 2005.

Iowa City native **Nate Kaeding (2000–2003)** was a consensus All-American and the winner of the 2002 Lou Groza Award, which goes to the nation's top kicker.

He is Iowa's all-time leading scorer with 373 points, and he ranks first in school history with 67 made field goals, including a school-record 22 in a row during the 2001 and 2002 seasons.

Kaeding earned All-Pro honors as a member of the San Diego Chargers in 2006.

Reggie Roby

Nate Kaeding

With his unique combination of intensity and homespun charm, Hayden Fry took a floundering Iowa football program and placed it on the national map.

The Coaches

The University of Iowa has had 25 head football coaches since the sport was established in 1889, but five truly stand out for their success at the school.

• **Howard Jones** has the distinction of putting both Iowa and Southern California in the national spotlight for the first time. Jones built Iowa into a national power in the early 1920s then did same thing at USC in the late 1920s and 1930s.

• **Dr. Eddie Anderson** took over an Iowa program in 1939 that had finished a combined 2–13–1 in the previous two seasons. All Anderson did in his inaugural season was lead Iowa to a 6–1–1 record and help Nile Kinnick win the Heisman Trophy.

• **Forest Evashevski** lifted Iowa to unprecedented success in the 1950s before retiring at the age 42 to be the school's athletic director.

• **Hayden Fry** took over an Iowa program in 1979 that had suffered through 17 consecutive non-winning seasons. He needed only three season to lead Iowa to the Rose Bowl.

• **Kirk Ferentz** finished 1–10 in his first season as the Iowa coach in 1999 and 11–2 in his fourth season. The Hawkeyes won at least 10 games in each season from 2002 to 2004 and won Big Ten titles in 2002 and 2004.

HOWARD JONES

1916–1923
Record at Iowa: 42–17–1 (8 seasons)
Big Ten titles: 1921, 1922

The University of Iowa supposedly took a risk in 1916 when it hired a young and inexperienced head coach named Howard Jones to a five-year contract worth $5,250 per year. The university never had made that kind of commitment to a coach, and Jones' background was iffy at best.

Jones got the job because his boyhood friend, Reed Lane, was an alumni representative on the Iowa Athletic Board. They both had attended the same prep school out east, but separated after going to college. Jones went to Yale; Lane to Iowa.

The Iowa Athletic Board was impressed with Jones' Ivy League background and his knowledge of the game. Jones was 30 years old when he was hired at Iowa.

His early years at Iowa were impacted by World War I, since many able-bodied men were in the military.

Iowa was respectable during those early years under Jones, but the program did suffer two embarrassing defeats, to Minnesota (67–0) in 1916 and to Nebraska (47–0) the next season. Interestingly, Nebraska never beat him again.

Jones suffered his only losing season as the Iowa coach in 1917 when the team finished 3–5.

The problems didn't last long, though, as the Hawkeyes finished 6–2–1 in 1918. Iowa held six of its nine opponents scoreless that season.

Things would only get better under Jones.

The Hawkeyes won 20 consecutive games between 1920 and 1923, and they finished undefeated in both the 1921 and 1922 seasons. Iowa also ended Notre Dame's 20-game winning steak in 1921 with a 10–7 victory.

The highlight to the 1922 season came when Iowa defeated Jones' alma mater Yale 6–0 in the second game. Yale was a national power at the time and was coached by Jones' brother, Tad Jones.

Nobody knew it at the time, but the 1923 season would be Jones' last season at Iowa. Tensions were mounting between Jones, who also served as athletic director, and the chairman of the athletic board, B.F. Lambert. The men had opposing views on consolidating athletics with physical education, and they disagreed over pay increases to the assistant coaches.

Making matters worse was the fact that Jones' wife wanted to move to a warmer climate. Jones eventually resigned at Iowa on February 29, 1924.

After coaching one year at Duke, Jones moved on to Southern California, where he achieved his greatest success and fame. Five of his USC teams were victorious in the Rose Bowl.

Jones died of a heart attack in 1941 in Los Angeles. He was considered one of the greatest college coaches of all time at the time of his death. And he is still the only coach to lead Iowa to back-to-back undefeated seasons.

© University of Iowa – CMP Photo Service

HOWARD JONES YEAR-BY-YEAR

YEAR	RECORD
1916	4–3
1917	3–5
1918	6–2–1
1919	5–2
1920	5–2
1921	7–0
1922	7–0
1923	5–3
Total	42–17–1

DR. EDDIE ANDERSON

1939–1942
1946–1949
Record at Iowa: 35–33–2

Dr. Eddie Anderson was in the midst of a spectacular run as the head coach at Holy Cross when the University of Iowa came calling after the 1938 season. Iowa had combined to win only 22 of 50 games from 1930 to 1938 and fans were getting restless.

Anderson initially wasn't interested in moving back to the Midwest—he was born in Oskaloosa, Iowa, and attended Notre Dame—but he eventually changed his mind. Anderson agreed to a three-year contract worth $10,000 annually.

Anderson was intrigued by the thought of coaching in the Big Ten, and he knew firsthand about Iowa's success under Howard Jones. Anderson was a star on the Notre Dame team that lost to Iowa in 1921. It was the only defeat Notre Dame suffered during his sophomore, junior and senior seasons.

Iowa never became a national power under Anderson's watch, but he did coach one of the greatest and most inspirational teams in school history.

The 1939 squad earned that distinction by finishing 6–1–1 in Anderson's debut season. The team was led by do-everything halfback Nile Kinnick and was called the "Ironmen" because most of the players never left the field.

Victories over national powers Notre Dame and Minnesota in consecutive weeks put Iowa on the national radar and Kinnick in the lead for the Heisman Trophy.

Kinnick would go on to win the Heisman Trophy in 1939, along with virtually every other individual award handed out that season. He credited Anderson for bringing the best out of him and his teammates.

Anderson was a very talented and focused man who performed surgeries in the morning then coached football in the afternoon. He attended high school in Mason City and played football at Notre Dame under Knute Rockne.

His last game as the Iowa coach was a 28–7 loss to Notre Dame in 1949.

EDDIE ANDERSON YEAR-BY-YEAR

YEAR	RECORD
1939	6–1–1
1940	4–4
1941	3–5
1942	6–4
1946	5–4
1947	3–5–1
1948	4–5
1949	4–5
Total	35–33–2

FOREST EVASHEVSKI

1952–1960
Record at Iowa: 52–27–4
Big Ten titles: 1956, 1958, 1960

On December 8, 1951, three men met in a corner of Gibby's restaurant in north Chicago to discuss the future of the Iowa football program. They weren't simply three ordinary men, but rather three men with connections and the power to effect change.

Two of the men seated at the table were Iowa athletic director Paul Brechler and athletic board chairman Paul Blommers. The third invited guest was Fritz Crisler, athletic director and long-time head coach at Michigan.

Iowa hadn't officially decided to make a coaching change at the time, but Brechler and Blommers wanted to discuss the overall status of the football program with Crisler.

During the course of the evening, Crisler brought up the name of one of his former Michigan players, Forest Evashevski.

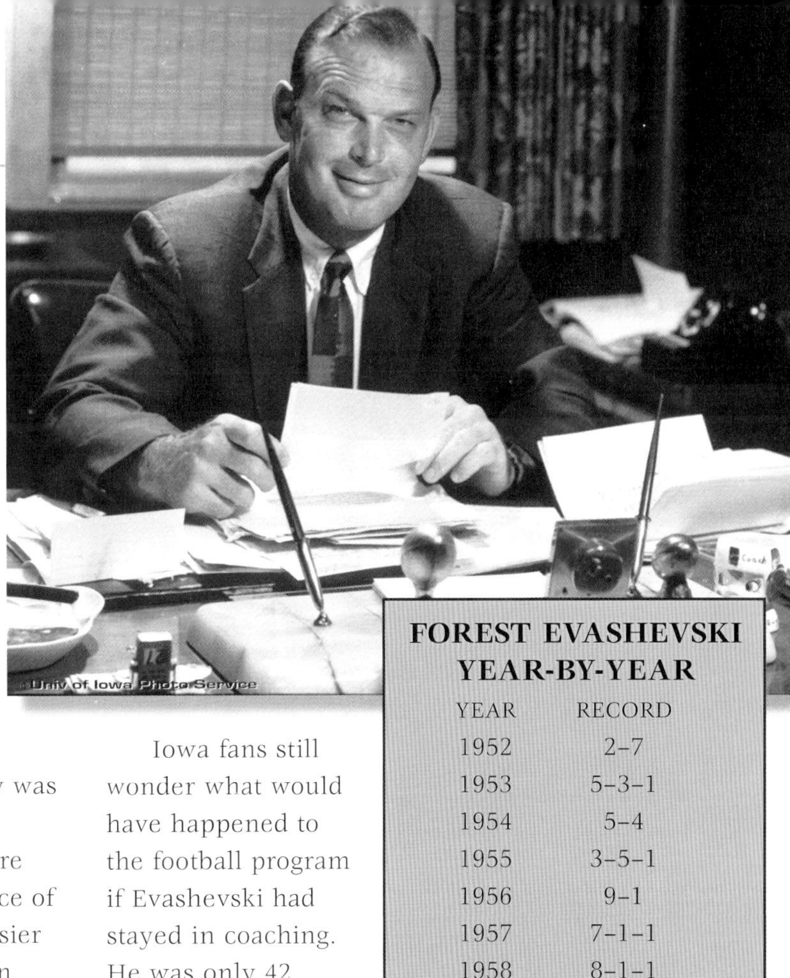

Evashevski was an All-Big Ten quarterback at Michigan and currently was the head coach at Washington State.

Indiana already was searching for a head coach and Evashevski was high on the list because he was eager to coach in the Big Ten.

Brechler called Evashevski shortly before Christmas in 1951 to discuss coaching at Iowa. Evashevski was hesitant at first because of the Indiana discussions, but he ultimately agreed to meet with Brechler, Blommers and Dr. Stuart Cullen at a secret gathering at a house in Denver, Colo. Both parties arrived by train and Evashevski reportedly was offered the Iowa job.

Evashevski mulled over both jobs before ultimately taking the Iowa job on the advice of Crisler. Evashevski felt that it would be easier to attain state-wide support in Iowa than in Indiana.

He accepted the job on January 6, 1952, replacing Leonard Raffensperger after only two seasons.

Crisler's recommendation paid huge dividends as Evashevski went on to become a coaching legend at Iowa. The Hawkeyes finished with a winning record in seven of the nine seasons that Evashevski coached. He is also the only coach to lead Iowa to a victory in the Rose Bowl. In fact, he did it twice, in 1957 and 1959.

Iowa combined to finish 24–3–2 during a three-season stretch from 1956 to 1958. Evashevski retired from coaching after leading Iowa to an 8–1 record in 1960.

He went out in style as Iowa defeated Notre Dame 28–0 in Evashevski's final game.

FOREST EVASHEVSKI YEAR-BY-YEAR

YEAR	RECORD
1952	2–7
1953	5–3–1
1954	5–4
1955	3–5–1
1956	9–1
1957	7–1–1
1958	8–1–1
1959	5–4
1960	8–1
Total	52–27–4

Iowa fans still wonder what would have happened to the football program if Evashevski had stayed in coaching. He was only 42 years old when he resigned to become the school's athletic director.

Evashevski was known as a tough, no-nonsense disciplinarian who struck fear in his players. He was bigger than many of his players, and he worked hard to stay in shape.

Evashevski was an avid racquetball player and many considered him the best in town during his time in Iowa City.

He also coached some of the best players in school history, including Outland Trophy winners Calvin Jones and Alex Karras and star quarterbacks Kenny Ploen and Randy Duncan.

Evashevski did color commentary for Iowa football games in the early 1980s and he currently lives in Michigan.

17

HAYDEN FRY

1979–1998

Record at Iowa: 143–89–6

Big Ten titles: 1981, 1985, 1990

Losing had become a way of life for Iowa fans when Hayden Fry accepted the challenge to rebuild the football program following the 1978 season. Bowl games were something that other schools, not Iowa, participated in at the end of season.

Iowa had suffered through 17 consecutive non-winning seasons when Fry arrived, and the previous four head coaches had lost their jobs trying to end the misery.

Things were different under Fry.

He already had rebuilt the programs at North Texas State and Southern Methodist when Iowa athletic director Bump Elliott began pursuing him.

Fry was impressed by the fan support after watching Iowa play on tape. He joked about how the fans went crazy when the team got a first down and wondered what they'd do if the Hawkeyes scored a touchdown.

Fry's sense of humor and his Texas drawl made him popular with Iowa fans, but his success made him a legend.

Fry also had a serious side that surfaced soon after he took the job. Iowa had just held its own during a 21–6 loss at Oklahoma in the second game of the 1979 season, and some of the players seemed satisfied with that.

But not Fry.

He warned the players afterward that he would smack anyone he saw smiling. His message was heard loud and clear.

Fry did the unimaginable by leading Iowa to the 1982 Rose Bowl in only his third season as head coach. He sustained his success by establishing recruiting pipelines throughout the country in his places like Texas and New Jersey.

And he led Iowa to a No. 1 ranking for six weeks in 1985.

Fry also is credited with breaking the stranglehold that Michigan and Ohio State had on the Big Ten during the 1970s. His wide-open passing attack was unusual for the Big Ten, and it took a while for teams to adjust. Some teams, like Wisconsin, never did.

Fry had a 15–2–1 record against Wisconsin, and his Iowa teams defeated Iowa State 15 consecutive times from 1983 to 1997.

Fry also coached seven All-Big Ten quarterbacks at Iowa, most notably Chuck Long, who finished runner-up to Bo Jackson for the 1985 Heisman Trophy.

The Hawkeyes played in 14 bowl games under Fry, including three Rose Bowls. Iowa had a 6–7–1 record in bowl games during Fry's tenure. Iowa also won at least eight games in 11 of Fry's 20 seasons as head coach.

Fry was inducted in the College Football Hall of Fame in 2004 and currently lives in Mesquite, Nevada, with his wife, Shirley.

Hayden Fry's Coaching Tree

Hayden Fry spent a career rebuilding struggling college football programs. And while doing so, Fry also helped launch the careers of some of today's most successful head coaches.

Fry's coaching tree includes his successor at Iowa, Kirk Ferentz, as well as Barry Alvarez, Bill Snyder, Bob Stoops, Mike Stoops, Bret Bielema, Chuck Long, Dan McCarney and Don Patterson among others.

Fry always said that he hired assistant coaches who aspired to be head coaches some day. Fry wanted his assistants to think that way, because he felt they would work harder to achieve their goals.

Ferentz coached the offensive line under Fry at Iowa from 1981 to 1989, whereas Snyder served as Fry's offensive coordinator from 1979 to 1988 before being hired at Kansas State. Snyder used much of what he learned under Fry to rebuild the Kansas State football program.

Snyder's rebuilding job at Kansas State ranks among the greatest reclamation projects in the history of college football.

Alvarez also took what he learned under Fry and used it to rebuild the Wisconsin football program. Alvarez then picked Bielema to be his successor, and it's hard to argue with the results, considering Wisconsin finished 12–1 in Bielema's debut season in 2006. Bielema walked on at Iowa while Fry was coaching, then joined Fry's staff as a graduate assistant.

Bob Stoops also served as a graduate assistant under Fry at Iowa before moving with Snyder to Kansas State.

"I consider them all like sons," Fry once said of his former assistant coaches. "I couldn't be more proud of what they've all accomplished."

HAYDEN FRY YEAR-BY-YEAR

YEAR	RECORD
1979	5–6
1980	4–7
1981	8–4
1982	8–4
1983	9–3
1984	8–4–1
1985	10–2
1986	9–3
1987	10–3
1988	6–4–3
1989	5–6
1990	8-4
1991	10–1–1
1992	5–7
1993	6–6
1994	5–5–1
1995	8–4
1996	9–3
1997	7–5
1998	3–8
Total	143–89–6

Celebrations were a common occurrence under Hayden Fry.

KIRK FERENTZ

1999–present
Record at Iowa: 55–43
Big Ten titles: 2002, 2004

Kirk Ferentz wasn't the popular choice to replace Hayden Fry as head coach, but that now seems hard to believe. Ferentz is one of the most highly respected and highest-paid college coaches in the country, pulling down nearly $3 million annually.

He earned his position by leading Iowa through a remarkable turnaround that caught virtually everybody, including the most devout fans, by surprise.

Many fans were screaming for Ferentz to go after Iowa finished 1–10 in his debut season in 1999. They were still upset about losing former Hawkeye player-turned-coach Bob Stoops to Oklahoma and took it out on Ferentz.

The situation got worse after Stoops led Oklahoma to the 2000 national title in his second season as head coach.

Iowa, meanwhile, finished 3–9 in 2000, but most felt the team was getting better. The Hawkeyes improved to 7–5 in 2001 and defeated Texas Tech in the Alamo Bowl.

Following the victory over Texas Tech, Ferentz stood on the victory stand inside the Alamodome and declared that the Hawkeyes were back.

Boy, was he right.

Iowa's resurgence under Ferentz became one of the biggest stories during the 2002 season. Led by an obscure quarterback named Brad Banks and a bunch of lightly recruited players, the Hawkeyes finished undefeated in the Big Ten for the first time in 80 years.

Banks finished runner-up for the 2002 Heisman Trophy, and former walk-on linebacker

Dallas Clark won the John Mackey Award, which goes to the nation's best tight end. Nate Kaeding also won the Lou Groza award in 2002 as the nation's top kicker.

Iowa set a school record for victories with 11 in 2002. The Hawkeyes also made their first and only appearance in a BCS bowl game that season, losing 38–17 to Southern California in the 2003 Orange Bowl.

Some critics still considered Iowa's rise a fluke until the Hawkeyes finished 10–3 in 2003 and 10–2 in 2004. It ranks as the greatest three-year stretch in school history in terms of victories.

Iowa has since come back down to earth, combining to finish just 13–12 during the 2005 and 2006 seasons.

But Ferentz is still considered a hot commodity among NFL executives. He spent six seasons as an NFL assistant coach before coming to Iowa.

Nothing Ferentz does is flashy, but he is meticulous and highly organized. It's not easy winning at Iowa because of the low population base in-state, but Ferentz has found a way to be successful.

He spent nine seasons as an Iowa assistant under Fry in the 1980s, but now Ferentz deserves to be mentioned in the same elite group with his former boss.

KIRK FERENTZ YEAR-BY-YEAR

YEAR	RECORD
1999	1–10
2000	3–9
2001	7–5
2002	11–2
2003	10–3
2004	10–2
2005	7–5
2006	6–7
Total	55–43

Two of the greatest moments in college football history: Iowa receiver Warren Holloway crosses the goal line to complete an improbable 56-yard TD that beats LSU 30–25 on the final play of the 2005 Capital One Bowl (above); Rob Houghtlin's kick as time expires allows top-ranked Iowa to beat second-ranked Michigan 12–10 in 1985 (right).

Hawkeye Superlatives

Warren Holloway became a Hawkeye legend the moment he crossed the goal line to defeat LSU on the final play of the 2005 Capital One Bowl. His stunning 56-yard yard touchdown pass from quarterback Drew Tate will forever be frozen in the minds of Iowa fans.

It was an incredible moment, but there are countless such moments that have created and sustained the aura of the Iowa football program.

After more than a century of football, here are 25 moments in Iowa football history that stand out. We've attempted to present them in order of magnitude, although each one carries with it a special set of circumstances and memories.

HOUGHTLIN BEATS MICHIGAN

Iowa 12, Michigan 10

October 19, 1985

Amid a fading, overcast sky and with the eyes of the nation watching, Rob Houghtlin did what every kicker dreams of doing. Houghtlin's 29-yard field goal as time expired lifted No. 1 Iowa past No. 2 Michigan 12–10 at Kinnick Stadium. Fans and players stormed the field afterward in a celebration that got so crazy that Iowa backup quarterback Mark Vlasic, who was the holder on field goals, injured his ankle during the celebration. This game is widely regarded as the greatest game in the history of Kinnick Stadium, and Houghtlin's kick is without question the most famous kick in school history.

COMING UP ROSES

Iowa 6, Ohio State 0

November 17, 1956

They always say the first time is the most special, and it was on this day that Iowa clinched its first trip to the Rose Bowl. Iowa broke a scoreless tie against defending national champion Ohio State in the third quarter when quarterback Kenny Ploen bootlegged to his left and found Jim Gibbons in the end zone for a 17-yard touchdown pass. Iowa's defense was incredible that day, not allowing the Buckeyes to advance beyond the Iowa 32-yard line.

MIRACLE IN THE MAGIC KINGDOM

Iowa 30, LSU 25

January 1, 2005

The situation looked hopeless when Iowa quarterback Drew Tate dropped back to throw a last-second desperation pass against LSU in the Capital One Bowl. Time was running out and the Iowa players looked confused and unorganized. Tate took the snap and dropped back in the pocket as the time on clock approached zero.

Meanwhile, Iowa receiver Warren Holloway, who had never caught a touchdown pass in college, had slipped behind the LSU secondary virtually unnoticed. Tate heaved the

Iowa clinched its first trip to the Rose Bowl with a 6-0 win over Ohio State in 1956.

Marv Cook made Hawkeye history with his 28-yard touchdown that gave Iowa a 29–27 win over Ohio State in 1987.

ball downfield and hit Holloway in stride. Holloway then broke free from a defender and covered the football with both hands as he ran into the end zone for the game-winning 56-yard touchdown catch.

Within seconds, he was snowed under by his teammates in the end zone. This would prove to be Nick Saban's final game as the LSU coach and the start of Holloway's legend.

COOK'S CATCH

Iowa 29, Ohio State 27
November 14, 1987

Nearly two decades before Warren Holloway made what many consider the greatest catch in school history, Iowa tight end Marv Cook made a similarly stunning play at the expense of Ohio State. The circumstances were virtually hopeless; trailing 27–22, Iowa was faced with a fourth-down-and-23 at the Ohio State 28-yard line, and the Hawkeyes had no timeouts left. Iowa quarterback Chuck Hartlieb threw a side-armed pass to Cook, who made the catch at the Ohio State 9-yard line near the right sideline. Cook spun away from one defender, then somehow carried two more defenders into the end zone, which he cleared by barely a foot. There were six seconds remaining when Cook scored to give Iowa a miraculous 29–27 win. Ohio State coach Earle Bruce was fired two days after the game.

The great Nile Kinnick almost single-handedly beat Notre Dame 7–6 in the classic 1939 encounter.

A LEGEND IS BORN

Iowa 7, Notre Dame 6

November 11, 1939

The legend of Nile Kinnick started to take shape on this day with a stunning 7–6 victory over Notre Dame. Iowa recovered a fumble at the Notre Dame 4-yard line, setting the stage for Kinnick to show off his football talent and wisdom. Kinnick normally lined up at left halfback, but he switched positions with Buzz Dean and lined up at right halfback, confusing the Notre Dame defenders. Kinnick took a direct snap from center and plowed into the end zone for a game-winning touchdown. He also drop-kicked the extra point, which proved to be the difference. A few weeks later, Kinnick was holding the Heisman Trophy.

CHANGING FORTUNES

Iowa 8, Ohio State 0

October 25, 1952

Coach Forest Evashevski gave Iowa fans a glimpse of the future when he coached the Hawkeyes past Ohio State 8–0 in his first season. It was one of only two wins on the season, which by all appearances was a failure. But this victory helped lay the foundation for Iowa's success in the 1950s, and it served notice that Evy was something special.

ONE FOR ONE IN PASADENA

Iowa 35, Oregon State 19

January 1, 1957

Iowa made its first appearance in the Rose Bowl a memorable one by pounding Oregon

State 35–19. Iowa shredded the Beavers with 408 total yards, including 301 yards courtesy of a pounding ground attack. Iowa quarterback Kenny Ploen rushed for 59 yards and passed for 83 more on his way to being named the game's most outstanding player. Ploen's 49-yard touchdown run opened the scoring.

MORE OF THE SAME

Iowa 38, California 12
January 1, 1959

The Hawkeyes were just as dominant in the Rose Bowl two years later. This time California was the overmatched opponent from the Pacific-8 Conference.

The Bears had no answer for Iowa's explosive rushing attack, which gained an incredible 429 yards during the 38–12 victory. Iowa halfback Bob Jeter gained 194 yards on only nine carries. Jeter gained nearly half his yards on an electrifying 81-yard touchdown run.

Fellow halfback Willie Fleming also scored two touchdowns for the Hawkeyes, who set a Rose Bowl record with 24 first downs.

HOSTILITIES RENEWED

Iowa 12, Iowa State 10
September 17, 1977

This day marked the renewal of the Iowa-Iowa State series, which had been dormant for 43 years. Iowa State was coming off an 8–3 season and was favored by three points even though the game was being played at Kinnick Stadium.

The Cyclones fully expected to win and emerged from the locker room wearing jerseys that said "Beat Iowa" on the front. But Iowa pulled the upset 12–10 in a game that featured plenty of hard hits, but few big plays, other than Dennis Mosley's 77-yard touchdown run for the Hawkeyes. All the scoring took place during a seven-and-a-half-minute period in the first and second quarters.

Iowa dominated California in the 1959 Rose Bowl.

FRY TURNS A CORNER

Iowa 9, Michigan 7
October 17, 1981

Hayden Fry's first signature win came in the Big House, and it was the key game in Iowa's first return to the Rose Bowl since 1959.

Iowa's march to the Big Ten title started gaining momentum with a 9–7 victory over Michigan in Ann Arbor. All of Iowa's points came on three field goals by kicker Tom Nichol. Michigan entered the game favored by two touchdowns and had a 22–4 record against Iowa at home, but things were starting to change in this rivalry.

A huge crowd gathered at the Cedar Rapids airport to welcome home their conquering heroes.

LONG GONE

Iowa 35, Michigan State 31
October 5, 1985

Iowa quarterback Chuck Long helped solidify his reputation for greatness by marching the Hawkeyes down the field in the closing seconds to defeat Michigan State 35–31. Long scored the game-winning touchdown from two yards out with 27 seconds left to play. He took the snap, then executed a superb fake handoff to running back Ronnie Harmon, who then leaped into the end zone. The Michigan State defenders seemed convinced that Harmon had the ball, because they all converged on him. Long then bootlegged to his right and jogged untouched into the end zone.

DOMINANCE IN ANN ARBOR

Iowa 34, Michigan 9
October 26, 2002

Iowa silenced the fans inside Michigan Stadium by crushing the Wolverines 34–9. It was Michigan's worst loss at home in 35 years and a key victory during Iowa's undefeated Big Ten campaign. Backup running back Jermelle Lewis rushed for over 100 yards and scored two touchdowns for Iowa.

ROSES FLOATED FROM THE SKY

Iowa 36, Michigan State 7
November 21, 1981

This was the day roses floated down from the press box at Kinnick Stadium. The roses were part of a wild post-game celebration following a 36–7 victory over Michigan State, which clinched Iowa's first berth in the Rose Bowl since the 1958 season. Ohio State had done the Hawkeyes a favor earlier in the day by defeating Michigan. The Iowa players heard the score of the Michigan game at halftime then went out and pounded the Spartans in the third and fourth quarters.

TITLE MARCH

Iowa 24, Michigan 23
October 20, 1990

Iowa's improbable march to the 1990 Big Ten title was helped immensely on this day with a 24–23 victory at Michigan. Linebacker John Derby helped to secure the victory by making an interception late in the game, which was the third of five consecutive Big Ten wins that carried the Hawkeyes to the title.

SERVING NOTICE

Iowa 10, Nebraska 7
September 12, 1981

The nation started to realize what Hayden Fry was doing as the Iowa coach when the Hawkeyes stunned sixth-ranked Nebraska 10–7 in the season-opener at home. The victory came almost a year after Nebraska had crushed Iowa 57–0 in Lincoln, Nebraska.

All-America punter Reggie Roby was huge for Iowa during the game, punting five times for a 55.8-yard average and flipping the field position time after time. The game was played in 90-degree temperatures. It was also was Fry's first signature victory as the Iowa coach.

FLEMING'S DAY

Iowa 37, Michigan 14
November 1, 1958

Willie Fleming only played one season at Iowa, but that was enough time for him to achieve stardom.

Fleming had perhaps his best game on this day when he carried the Hawkeyes past Michigan 37–14. It was Iowa's first win at Michigan in 34 years. The fact that Fleming grew up in Detroit made the victory that much sweeter. Fleming finished with 240 total yards, including a 72-yard punt return for a touchdown.

WOODSHED WHIPPING

Iowa 37, Florida 17
January 1, 2004

The Hawkeyes entered the Outback Bowl as a decisive underdog to Florida, but it was hard to tell when the game started. Iowa dominated its speedy opponent from the SEC and rolled to a 37–17 victory. Fred Russell danced for 150 yards and a touchdown on 21 carries, and the defense stifled the Chris Leak-led Gator offense.

Kirk Ferentz became the first Iowa coach since Forest Evashevski to win a bowl game in January.

Kirk Ferentz (below) and Chad Greenway (right) were hardly intimidated by the big, bad Gators in the 2004 Outback Bowl.

HANGING ON

Iowa 42, Penn State 35
September 28, 2002

The dream season almost turned into a nightmare in Happy Valley. Iowa jumped out to a 35–13 fourth-quarter lead, only to have Penn State score 22 fourth-quarter points and force the game into overtime. The Hawkeyes kept their composure and escaped from Happy Valley with a 42–35 victory in front of more than 108,000 hostile fans. Brad Banks and Fred Russell were the dynamic duo, combining for 344 yards of offense. And the improbable march to a Big Ten title continued unabated.

SHINING IN THE SUN

Iowa 38, Washington 18
December 29, 1995

This marked another time that Iowa thrived as an underdog in a bowl game. Junior running back Sedrick Shaw led the charge as the Hawkeyes pounded Washington 38–18 in the Sun Bowl. Washington was co-champs of the Pac-10, whereas Iowa had lost four consecutive games at one point during the regular season. But the Shaw-Tavian Banks combination was too much for the Huskies. Shaw rushed for 135 yards while Banks added 122.

Fred Russell left Nittany Lion defenders grasping at air during the Hawkeyes' awesome offensive show against Penn State in 2002.

BOILING OVER

Iowa 31, Purdue 28
October 5, 2002

Iowa's 31–28 victory over Purdue featured one momentum shift after another and numerous big plays. All-America tight end Dallas Clark caught what proved to be the game-winning touchdown from Brad Banks in the final minutes of the fourth quarter. But it wasn't until reserve defensive back Adolphous Shelton intercepted a pass in the closing seconds that Iowa fans could celebrate the victory at Kinnick Stadium.

JUST PEACHY

Iowa 28, Tennessee 22
December 31, 1982

Iowa defeated Tennessee 28–22 in the Peach Bowl to give Hayden Fry his first bowl victory thanks to the brilliance of quarterback Chuck Long. Long completed 14 of 17 first-half passes for 231 yards and three touchdowns as the Hawkeyes built a 21–7 halftime lead. The second half turned tense for Iowa, but the Hawkeyes held on. Long passed for a Peach Bowl-record 304 yards in the 28–22 win.

DELIRIOUS DAY IN HAPPY VALLEY

Iowa 42, Penn State 34
September 17, 1983

Iowa did more than just beat Penn State 42–34 on this day; it built momentum for a dominant run of excellence. The 42 points were the most points ever scored by an opponent at Penn State. The game helped launch the careers of Iowa quarterback Chuck Long and running back Ronnie Harmon to All-America status.

TURNING POINT

Iowa 26, Penn State 23
November 4, 2000

There is a turning point in every rebuilding phase, and this is where Kirk Ferentz says the Hawkeyes started heading in the right direction on his watch. Defensive back Ryan Hansen made an interception to secure a 26–23 double-overtime victory in Happy Valley in yet another memorable day at Penn State's Beaver Stadium.

TITLE TIME

Iowa 29, Minnesota 27
November 13, 2004

Iowa hung on to win at Minnesota 29–27 and clinched at least a share of the Big Ten title. It was the sixth of what turned out to be a season-closing eight-game winning streak, as the Hawkeyes posted their third straight season with at least 10 wins.

LAST LAUGH

Iowa 21, Penn State 20
October 19, 1996

This game marked the last time that Hayden Fry and Joe Paterno faced each other as head coaches. Fry got the last laugh as the Hawkeyes escaped from rain-soaked Happy Valley with a 21–20 victory.

Do-everything receiver-returner Tim Dwight was the star for Iowa, returning a punt for a touchdown and setting up another score with a spectacular over-the-head catch. Tavian Banks also rushed for over 100 yards while subbing for an injured Sedrick Shaw.

REMEMBER THE ALAMO

Iowa 19, Texas Tech 16
December 29, 2001

Iowa defeated Texas Tech 19–16 to give Kirk Ferentz his first bowl victory. Two names that will live in Iowa lore—Nick Kaeding and Bob Sanders—clinched the win for the Hawkeyes. Kaeding kicked a 47-yard field goal with 44 seconds to go, and Sanders intercepted a Texas Tech pass in the end zone on the final play of the game. Kaeding tied an Iowa record with four field goals, while Sanders added 11 tackles to his interception.

GOOD THINGS BRUIN

Iowa 21, UCLA 10
September 21, 1974

There weren't many highlights during the Bob Commings coaching regime at Iowa, but one of the biggest came in his second game at the helm. Iowa defeated UCLA 21–10 for one of the biggest wins during the Commings era. Dick Vermeil coached an established UCLA program at the time. It was one of only three wins that season.

Colin Cole celebrates the first bowl win of the Ferentz era: a 19–16 Alamo Bowl triumph over Texas Tech.

SYLVANIA
SYLVANIA
ALAMOBOWL
94

1921 (7–0–0)

Coach: Howard Jones
Iowa 52, Knox 14,
Iowa 10, Notre Dame 7
Iowa 14, Illinois 2
Iowa 13, Purdue 6
Iowa 41, Minnesota 7
Iowa 41, Indiana 0
Iowa 14, Northwestern 0

Many considered Iowa's undefeated 1921 squad as the best in nation that season. The first-, second- and fourth-leading scorers in the Big Ten in 1921 were all Hawkeyes. This team also stopped Notre Dame's 20-game winning streak and held all but one opponent to seven points or less. Iowa's 41–7 victory over Minnesota marked the most points ever scored against the Gophers up to that time.

This team featured a number of Hawkeye legends, most notably quarterback Aubrey Devine, lineman Duke Slater, fullback Gordon Locke and end Lester Belding. Devine scored a combined 57 points in back-to-back victories over Minnesota and Indiana.

Rumors surfaced after the season that Iowa was looking to play a postseason game. Coach Howard Jones was called into a conference with a committee representing the California Tournament of Roses Association to discuss the possibility of Iowa playing one of the top teams from the Pacific Coast on New Year's Day. The game never happened, though, because the Iowa Board of Regents opposed postseason competition at the time, and the Big Ten had adopted a ruling six months earlier that prevented such a thing from happening. So the Hawkeyes were denied one final chance to prove their national supremacy.

1922 (7–0–0)

Coach: Howard Jones
Iowa 61, Knox 0
Iowa 6, Yale 0
Iowa 8, Illinois 7
Iowa 56, Purdue 0
Iowa 28, Minnesota 14
Iowa 12, Ohio State 9
Iowa 37, Northwestern 3

Iowa suffered significant personnel losses from the previous season, but that didn't stop the 1922 squad from also finishing undefeated. Gordon Locke scored four times in the season-opener against Knox, and the Hawkeyes finished with 471 rushing yards in the rout.

Iowa then took part in one of the classic games of that era the next week against Yale. Not only was Yale a national power, but it was also coached by Howard Jones' brother Tad Jones. It was only the second time in collegiate football history that two brothers had faced each other as opposing coaches. Howard earned family bragging rights as the Hawkeyes held on for a 6–0 victory.

Iowa held three opponents scoreless in 1922, and no opponent scored more than 14 points against the Hawkeyes. Locke had a tremendous game against Ohio State, scoring both of Iowa's touchdowns and rushing for 126 yards during a 12–9 victory. Many considered Iowa to be the top team in the nation by season's end. Iowa, Princeton and California were the only teams to finish undefeated that season.

1939 Hawkeyes

1956 Hawkeyes

1939 (6–1–1)

Coach: Eddie Anderson
Iowa 41, South Dakota 0
Iowa 32, Indiana 29,
Michigan 27, Iowa 7
Iowa 19, Wisconsin 13
Iowa 4, Purdue 0
Iowa 7, Notre Dame 6
Iowa 13, Minnesota 9
Iowa 7, Northwestern 7

Hawkeye fans were tired of losing and were still coping with the Great Depression when Nile Kinnick and the Ironmen finally gave them something to cheer about. Dr. Eddie Anderson, an Iowa native and a former player under Knute Rockne at Notre Dame, was hired as the Iowa head coach before the 1939 season. The change had a dramatic and immediate impact as the Hawkeyes finished 6–1–1 and defeated national powers Notre Dame and Minnesota in back-to-back games. Iowa had combined to win only two games in the previous two seasons.

Kinnick became a star on the national level, and his senior season culminated with his winning the 1939 Heisman Trophy and virtually every other individual award. The team earned its nickname as the Ironmen, as most of the players rarely left the field during games.

1956 (9–1)

Coach: Forest Evashevski
Iowa 27, Indiana 0
Iowa 14, Oregon State 13
Iowa 13, Wisconsin 7
Iowa 34, Hawaii 0
Iowa 21, Purdue 20
Michigan 17, Iowa 14
Iowa 7, Minnesota 0
Iowa 6, Ohio State 0
Iowa 48, Notre Dame 8
Iowa 35, Oregon State 19 (Rose Bowl)

Most prognosticators picked Iowa to finish near the bottom of the Big Ten in 1956, but they weren't aware of the change in offensive philosophy that had taken place during the spring practice. Iowa coach Forest Evashevski installed a new wing-T offense that would prove highly effective throughout his reign.

Marked by ball fakes and numerous bootlegs, the new offense helped Iowa climb all the way to No. 3 in the rankings in 1956.

The Hawkeyes started quickly in the season opener against Indiana, with touchdown marches of 82 and 69 yards in the first quarter. Iowa's new wing-T formation produced 242 rushing yards during a 27–0 victory. Iowa won its first five games before losing to Michigan 17–14. The Hawkeyes closed the regular season with victories over Minnesota, Ohio State and Notre Dame. The 6–0 victory over Ohio State helped clinch the first Rose Bowl appearance in school history.

Iowa then crushed Notre Dame by 40 points in the regular-season finale, setting the stage for the Rose Bowl.

Senior quarterback Kenny Ploen starred as Iowa overpowered Oregon State in the Rose Bowl. Iowa's wing-T offense accounted for 408 total yards, including 301 on the ground. The defense also did its part that season by shutting out four opponents.

1958 (8–1–1)

Coach: Forest Evashevski
Iowa 17, TCU 0
Iowa 13, Air Force 13
Iowa 34, Indiana 13
Iowa 20, Wisconsin 9
Iowa 26, Northwestern 20
Iowa 37, Michigan 14
Iowa 28, Minnesota 6
Ohio State 38, Iowa 28
Iowa 31, Notre Dame 21
Iowa 38, California 12 (Rose Bowl)

Some still consider this star-studded squad as the best team in school history. You name it and this team had it—from scintillating playmakers on offense to dominant defensive players to a star quarterback. Bob Jeter and Willie Fleming were capable of scoring from anywhere on the field, and they provided Iowa with an explosive one-two punch at running back. But if you focused too much on them, then quarterback Randy Duncan would make you pay. Duncan finished second in the voting for the 1958 Heisman Trophy.

One of the high points in the season came when Iowa crushed Michigan 37–14 in Ann Arbor. The victory was especially sweet for Evashevski, because he grew up in Michigan and played for the Wolverines.

Iowa capped the season by routing California in the Rose Bowl. Jeter rushed for 194 yards in the Rose Bowl and Fleming scored two touchdowns for the fifth consecutive game. Iowa finished with 515 total yards, including 429 rushing yards. Following the Rose Bowl, Iowa won the Grantland Rice Award, which was similar to winning the national championship at the time. This season also capped a three-year stretch during which Iowa finished 24–3–2 while using the wing-T offense.

1981
(8–4, 6–2 BIG TEN)

Coach: Hayden Fry
Iowa 10, Nebraska 7
Iowa State 23, Iowa 12
Iowa 20, UCLA 7
Iowa 64, Northwestern 0
Iowa 42, Indiana 28
Iowa 9, Michigan 7
Minnesota 12, Iowa 10
Illinois 24, Iowa 7
Iowa 33, Purdue 7
Iowa 17, Wisconsin 7
Iowa 36, Michigan State 7
Washington 28, Iowa 0 (Rose Bowl)

Hayden Fry's third team at Iowa helped break the stranglehold that Michigan and Ohio State had held on the Big Ten for over a decade. Nobody expected much from the Hawkeyes in 1981; Iowa had finished only 4–7 the previous season. But the players were sick and tired of losing, and the defense, led by all-America end Andre Tippett, had star potential.

Iowa served notice immediately by shocking Nebraska 10–7 in the season opener at home; the Huskers had crushed Iowa 57–0 a year earlier. Following a disappointing loss to Iowa State in the second game, Iowa pulled off another upset in week 3 by defeating UCLA 20–7. The nation started taking Fry's boys seriously when they upset Michigan 9–7 on the road. Tom Nichol scored all of Iowa's points on three field goals. The Hawkeyes hit a roadblock with back-to-back losses to Minnesota and Illinois, but then bounced back to win the final three regular-season games.

One of the more memorable moments in school history came when Iowa defeated Michigan State in the regular-season finale to clinch a spot in the Rose Bowl for the first time in 23 years. Washington blanked Iowa in the Rose Bowl, but the loss didn't diminish what this team accomplished.

1985 (10–2, 7–1 BIG TEN)

Coach: Hayden Fry
Iowa 58, Drake 0
Iowa 48, Northern Illinois 20
Iowa 57, Iowa State 3
Iowa 35, Michigan State 31
Iowa 23, Wisconsin 13
Iowa 12, Michigan 10
Iowa 49, Northwestern 10
Ohio State 22, Iowa 13
Iowa 59, Illinois 0
Iowa 27, Purdue 24
Iowa 31, Minnesota 9
UCLA 45, Iowa 28 (Rose Bowl)

Iowa became a national contender in 1985 the moment Chuck Long decided to return for his senior season instead of leaving for the NFL. This team was similar to Iowa's 1958 squad in that it had stars on both offense and defense and a quarterback who finished runner-up for the Heisman Trophy.

Iowa won its first seven games and was ranked No. 1 in the nation for five weeks during the season. The Hawkeyes defeated Michigan 12–10 in a game in which Iowa entered ranked No. 1 and Michigan No. 2 in the country. Ohio State ended Iowa's chance for an undefeated season, though, with a 22–13 victory on a rain-soaked day in Columbus in the eighth game.

One of Iowa's best and most dominant performances came at the expense of Illinois. Iowa led the Illini 49–0 at halftime and cruised to a 59–0 victory.

The season ended sadly, though, as Iowa self-destructed during a 45–28 loss to UCLA in the Rose Bowl. All-America halfback Ronnie Harmon drew the ire of Hawkeye fans by fumbling four times in the game.

Long was a consensus All-American, and he finished runner-up to Auburn running back Bo Jackson for the 1985 Heisman Trophy by the narrowest margin in the award's history. Long, Harmon and offensive lineman Mike Haight were all taken in the first round of the 1986 draft.

1990 (8–4, 6–2 BIG TEN)

Coach: Hayden Fry
Iowa 63, Cincinnati 10
Iowa 45, Iowa State 35
Miami (Florida) 48, Iowa 21
Iowa 12, Michigan State 7
Iowa 30, Wisconsin 10
Iowa 24, Michigan 23
Iowa 56, Northwestern 14
Iowa 54, Illinois 28
Ohio State 27, Iowa 26
Iowa 38, Purdue 9
Minnesota 31, Iowa 24
Washington 46, Iowa 34 (Rose Bowl)

This team proved its doubters wrong by winning the Big Ten title only a year after having a losing season. Led by running backs Nick Bell and Tony Stewart and quarterback Matt Rodgers, Iowa featured a balanced offense and a hard-hitting, opportunistic defense.

The Hawkeyes bounced back from a 48–21 loss at Miami (Florida) in the third game of the season to win their next five games, including a 24–23 victory at Michigan. Iowa had perhaps its best performance of the season during a stunning 54–28 victory at Illinois, which was ranked in the top 10 at the time. Bell was named the Big Ten's most valuable player, and Rodgers also made first-team all-conference.

The defense was led by All-Big Ten linebacker Melvin Foster and defensive back Merton Hanks, who went on to star for the San Francisco 49ers.

Iowa fell behind Washington 33–7 in the Rose Bowl, but stormed back to make the final score respectable at 46–34.

1991 (10–1–1, 7–1 BIG TEN)

Coach: Hayden Fry
Iowa 53, Hawaii 10
Iowa 29, Iowa State 10
Iowa 58, Northern Illinois 7
Michigan 43, Iowa 24
Iowa 10, Wisconsin 6
Iowa 24, Illinois 21
Iowa 31, Purdue 21
Iowa 16, Ohio State 9
Iowa 38, Indiana 21
Iowa 24, Northwestern 10
Iowa 23, Minnesota 8
Iowa 13, Brigham Young 13 (Holiday Bowl)

This team didn't win the Big Ten title due to its loss to Michigan, and it tied its bowl game, but it was victorious against every other opponent. Matt Rodgers made first-team All-Big Ten for the second consecutive season, and defensive end Leroy Smith earned consensus All-America honors.

This season marked the third time under Hayden Fry that Iowa won 10 games.

2002 (11–2, 8–0 BIG TEN)

Coach: Kirk Ferentz
Iowa 57, Akron 21
Iowa 29, Miami (Ohio) 24
Iowa State 36, Iowa 31
Iowa 48, Utah State 7
Iowa 42, Penn State 35 (OT)
Iowa 31, Purdue 28
Iowa 44, Michigan State 16
Iowa 24, Indiana 8
Iowa 34, Michigan 9
Iowa 20, Wisconsin 3
Iowa 62, Northwestern 10
Iowa 45, Minnesota 21
Southern California 38, Iowa 17 (Orange Bowl)

The 2002 edition of the Hawkeyes remains the only team in school history to win 11 games and to play in a BCS bowl game. It was also the first Iowa team in 80 years to finish undefeated in the Big Ten. Not bad considering Iowa was picked to finish in the lower division of the Big Ten in 2002.

The Hawkeyes had several players who went from being no-names to stars during the course of the season. The catalyst was senior quarterback Brad Banks, who went from being a reserve in 2001 to finishing as the runner-up for the Heisman Trophy in 2002. Banks passed for 2,573 yards and 26 touchdowns during the season. He also caused defenses fits with his running. Junior tight end Dallas Clark won the John Mackey Award, given to the nation's top tight end, and junior Nate Kaeding won the Lou Groza Award, given to the top kicker in college football.

Iowa also featured what many felt was the best offensive line in the Big Ten and perhaps the country. This team showed its resiliency by overcoming a devastating loss to Iowa State at home in the third game to win nine games in a row. The Hawkeyes weren't able to overcome Carson Palmer and USC in the Orange Bowl, though, losing 38–17. But that game did little to diminish what the Hawkeyes accomplished.

2002 Hawkeyes

2003
(10–3, 5–3 BIG TEN)

Coach: Kirk Ferentz
Iowa 21, Miami (Ohio) 3
Iowa 56, Buffalo 7
Iowa 40, Iowa State 21
Iowa 21, Arizona State 2
Michigan State 20, Iowa 10
Iowa 30, Michigan 27
Ohio State 19, Iowa 10
Iowa 26, Penn State 14
Iowa 41, Illinois 10
Purdue 27, Iowa 14
Iowa 40, Minnesota 22
Iowa 27, Wisconsin 21
Iowa 37, Florida 17 (Outback Bowl)

Iowa was expected to suffer a drop-off after losing so many star players from the 2002 team. But this team just found a way to win games that it probably had no business winning. Nathan Chandler, a 6'7" junior-college transfer, made the most of his only season as the starting quarterback. He struggled at times, but he played big in big games. Chandler was named the MVP of the Outback Bowl, a resounding 37–17 win over Florida. Senior left tackle Robert Gallery won the 2003 Outland Trophy, given to the nation's top offensive lineman, and was selected second overall by the Oakland Raiders in the 2004 NFL draft.

2004
(10–2, 7–1 BIG TEN)

Coach: Kirk Ferentz
Iowa 39, Kent State 7
Iowa 17, Iowa State 10
Arizona State 44, Iowa 7
Michigan 30, Iowa 17
Iowa 38, Michigan State 16
Iowa 33, Ohio State 7
Iowa 6, Penn State 4
Iowa 23, Illinois 13
Iowa 23, Purdue 21
Iowa 29, Minnesota 27
Iowa 30, Wisconsin 7
Iowa 30, Louisiana State 25 (Capital One Bowl)

The Hawkeyes overcame a 44–7 loss at Arizona State in the third game and a lackluster 2–2 start to win 10 games for the sixth time in school history. The fact that Iowa accomplished that feat while barely boasting anything resembling a rushing attack is what made this team so special.

Drew Tate burst on the scene to earn first-team All-Big Ten honors as a sophomore quarterback. He capped the season by throwing arguably the greatest touchdown pass in school history to Warren Holloway on the final play of the 2005 Capital One Bowl, a 30–25 win over LSU. He also shredded Ohio State for over 300 yards passing during a 33–7 drubbing at Kinnick Stadium. Iowa had to rely on Tate's passing after the top three running backs suffered season-ending knee injuries. Walk-on Sam Brownlee began the season buried on the depth chart at running back, but he was a key performer down the stretch. His presence gave Iowa a semblance of balance on offense. The defense was dominant throughout the season and featured arguably the best line in the country, led by end Matt Roth and tackle Jonathon Babineaux.

Iowa's Dennis Mosley tries to elude a Minnesota defender during the 1976 battle for the Floyd of Rosedale Trophy.

The Rivalries

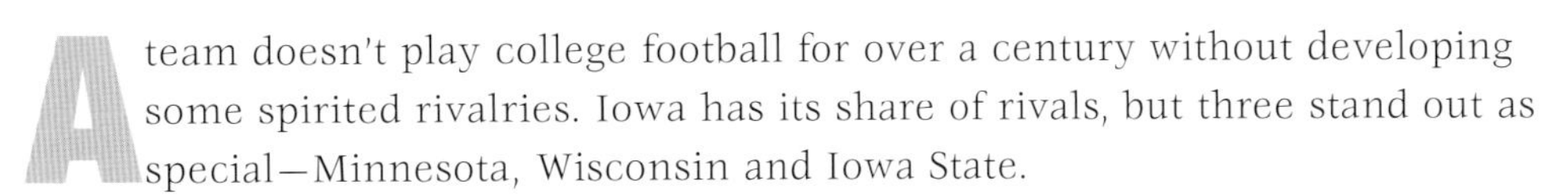

A team doesn't play college football for over a century without developing some spirited rivalries. Iowa has its share of rivals, but three stand out as special—Minnesota, Wisconsin and Iowa State.

It wouldn't be a typical season if the Hawkeyes didn't play one of those three teams. The Cyclones and Hawkeyes compete for in-state bragging rights, whereas border supremacy is at stake whenever Iowa faces Minnesota or Wisconsin.

Iowa also has a long history of competing against Purdue and a competitive history with Michigan State and Michigan.

Here is a closer look at each series.

IOWA VS. MINNESOTA

Iowa trails 39–59–2

For the past 70 years, Iowa and Minnesota have played for the right to keep a statue of a pig named Floyd of Rosedale on the winner's campus.

It sounds sort of corny, but the circumstances that led to Floyd's creation in the mid-1930s were serious and sad. Floyd came to be as a result of racism.

Iowa fans were upset with how star halfback Ozzie Simmons had been treated by the Minnesota players during the 1934 game in Minneapolis. Tensions were still high a year later as the teams prepared to face each other again.

Simmons was one of the few black players in the Big Ten at the time. But he was more than just a black player; he was a star, and the Gophers didn't like it, nor did their fans.

With the 1935 game approaching, Governor Floyd B. Olson of Minnesota and Governor Clyde Herring of Iowa made a friendly wager on the outcome of the game. The bet was considered an act of diplomacy and was intended to ease the friction between the two schools. The prize that was at stake? The original Floyd, a full-blooded champion hog.

Following Minnesota's 13–6 victory, Herring had the live hog shipped to Olson in Minnesota.

The Minnesota governor then presented it to the University of Minnesota, after commissioning Charles Brieschi, a St. Paul sculptor, to create a bronze likeness of the hog. The trophy is 21 inches long and 151½ inches high and weighs 94 pounds.

It was first presented in 1936 a year after the Gophers won the real thing.

Floyd's popularity helps to explain the passion and fervor behind rivalries.

If you were to rank Iowa's biggest rivals, Minnesota would be on top followed probably by Wisconsin and Iowa State.

Notre Dame used to be a huge rival for Iowa, and in some ways still is, even though the teams haven't faced each other since the 1960s.

Minnesota and Wisconsin, on the other hand, are fixtures on the Iowa schedule. In fact, Iowa and Minnesota have a long tradition of facing each other in the final regular season game.

Fans from both schools always look forward to the annual road trip, whether it is north to Minneapolis or south to Iowa City.

Minnesota in recent years has played the role of spoiler against Iowa, but there was a time when the Gophers dominated the series. Iowa has a 17–8 record against Minnesota since 1982, but the Gophers still have a 59–39–2 advantage overall.

Minnesota won the first 12 games in the series, including the inaugural contest 42–4 in 1891. The Gophers also won 13 of 14 games in the series from 1931 to 1944.

Minnesota was a national power in the 1930s and 1940s under legendary coach Bernie Bierman, whereas Iowa struggled during most of those years.

Things changed during the 1950s, when Iowa become a national power under Coach Forest Evashevski.

Iowa defeated the Gophers six times during a seven-year stretch from 1953 to 1959, including five times in a row.

Minnesota regained the upper hand during the 1960s and held it until Hayden Fry arrived nearly two decades later. The Gophers compiled a 17–4–1 record in the series from 1960 to 1981.

Iowa then defeated Minnesota 21–16 on October 23, 1982 in Minneapolis and has dominated the series for the most part ever since.

Minnesota's 34–24 victory in 2006 marked only the eighth time since 1982 that it has defeated Iowa.

The series has featured its share of upsets at the expense of both schools.

Nile Kinnick starred in perhaps the greatest upset in 1939 when the Hawkeyes shocked Minnesota 13–9 at home.

Iowa already had upset Notre Dame 7–6 the previous week, so hopes were high heading into the Minnesota game.

However, Minnesota was leading 9–0 in the fourth quarter when Kinnick led an improbable comeback. He threw two touchdown passes in the fourth quarter and played the entire 60 minutes.

Kinnick emerged from those two upset victories as the overwhelming favorite to win the 1939 Heisman Trophy, which he ultimately did in December.

Iowa players hoist the Floyd of Rosedale trophy after defeating Minnesota 42–24, November 17, 2001.

The circumstances were much different when Iowa faced the Gophers in 1990 in Minneapolis. Iowa already had clinched a spot in the Rose Bowl, but that didn't stop the Gophers from pulling off a 31–24 upset.

Iowa has held Minnesota scoreless eight times in the series, the most recent being a 31–0 victory in 1997 at Kinnick Stadium.

Minnesota has held Iowa scoreless 18 times in the series, but not since 1967. Iowa failed to score a point in six of the first seven games against the powerful Gophers.

Iowa's worst defeat in the series was a 75–0 drubbing in 1903 in Minneapolis. Iowa's biggest win came by a 61–10 margin in 1983 at home.

One of the more memorable games for Iowa fans occurred in 2002 when the Hawkeyes clinched their first undefeated Big Ten season in 80 years against Minnesota. The Metrodome turned into Iowa's home away from home that day. Fans paraded around in the stands and tore down one of the goal posts then tried unsuccessfully to carry it out of the building.

Iowa had to reimburse the Minnesota athletic department $5,000 for the cost of the goal post. A small price to pay for a lasting memory from this memorable series.

Bill Anderson holds the Badgers at bay.

IOWA VS. WISCONSIN

Series tied 40–40–2

Iowa's rivalry with Wisconsin didn't need a spark, but it recently got one when Bret Bielema was hired to coach the Badgers.

Wisconsin finished 12–1 in Bielema's first season in 2006, making him the only Badger coach to win 12 games in a season.

Bielema is also almost certainly the only Wisconsin head coach ever to sport a tattoo of an Iowa tiger hawk on his calf. Bielema got the tattoo as a tribute to his playing days at Iowa, where he walked on as a defensive lineman in 1988 and grew to become a team captain.

Bielema is proud of his roots, as are all the players from both teams in this spirited border rivalry.

The Iowa-Wisconsin game is something that fans from both schools look forward to each year. It also has been highly competitive, considering the series is tied at 40–40–2 overall.

It makes sense that Wisconsin is one of Iowa's biggest rivals because the campuses are less than 200 miles from each other.

The schools also recruit many of the same players from the Midwest.

Iowa played Wisconsin for the first time in 1894 and lost 44–0 in Madison, Wisconsin. The Badgers actually won the first six games in the series, including three by shutouts.

Iowa recorded its first victory over Wisconsin on November 15, 1924, in Madison by a 21–7 margin. The Hawkeyes recorded their first shutout in the series three years later with a 16–0 victory in 1927.

Much like the series with Minnesota, the Badgers dominated Iowa during the early years and during most of the 1960s and 1970s.

Hayden Fry's arrival in 1979 shifted the balance of power to Iowa's side. He won 15 of his first 16 games against the Badgers, with the only blemish being a 10–10 tie in 1984.

In fact, Iowa went 18 consecutive games from 1977 to 1996 without losing to Wisconsin.

The Badgers finally broke through in 1997 by defeating Iowa 13–10 at home.

Iowa fans like to say that it took a former Hawkeye assistant to end the misery. Former Wisconsin coach Barry Alvarez got his big break when Fry hired him as part of his original staff at Iowa in 1979. Alvarez had just led Mason City (Iowa) High School to a state title when Fry hired him.

Part of his rebuilding job at Wisconsin, besides winning three Big Ten titles and three Rose Bowls, was ending Iowa's dominance in the series.

Wisconsin defeated Iowa in 1998, 1999, 2000 and 2001 by a combined score of 119–38.

The Hawkeyes reversed the trend in 2002 with a 20–3 victory at Kinnick Stadium. That was the start of a four-game winning streak for Iowa against Wisconsin that ended in 2006 when Bielema defeated his alma mater.

The Badgers gained a measure of revenge, because Iowa had spoiled Alvarez's farewell ceremony at Camp Randall Stadium the year before. Wisconsin fans were in a celebratory mood on Nov. 12, 2005, but it didn't last long as Iowa came from behind to beat the Badgers 20–10 in Alvarez's final regular-season game as head coach.

The series also added a new feature when the Heartland Trophy was introduced in 2004. The trophy goes to the winning team each year.

The trophy was designed and crafted by artist and former Iowa player Frank Strub. The trophy features a bull mounted on a walnut base and has been inscribed with the scores of all the games in the series. The next score to be inscribed will break the tie in this hotly contested series.

When blocking a Hawkeye, just grab and hold on for dear life.

IOWA VS. IOWA STATE

Iowa leads 36–18

One of the most anticipated days in Iowa each fall is the Saturday when the Hawkeyes and Cyclones square off in football.

Fans from both schools circle the calendar to mark this annual showdown, especially since Iowa State became competitive over the past decade.

The Cyclones have won six of the last nine games in the series dating back to 1998.

Former Iowa player and coach Dan McCarney lasted 12 seasons as the Iowa State head coach despite having a losing record. McCarney lasted mostly because he beat his alma mater five consecutive times from 1998 to 2002.

Iowa still has a commanding lead in the series, and fans can thank Hayden Fry for that. His Iowa teams defeated Iowa State 15 consecutive times from 1983 to 1997, and some by huge margins.

Fry used to toy with the Cyclone faithful by saying they put too much emphasis on the Iowa game. He was convinced that the Iowa State players and coaches would get so pumped up for the Iowa game that they would let it affect the rest of their season.

The truth is that Iowa simply had better talent during its run of dominance in the 1980s and 1990s.

Iowa State is at a disadvantage in a number of ways compared to Iowa. The Cyclones don't have Iowa's tradition or resources or fan base when it comes to football.

There was a time when Iowa State couldn't even convince Iowa to play it in football. The series was inactive from 1935 to 1976. Many Hawkeye fans preferred it that way, because they felt Iowa had nothing to gain and everything to lose by playing Iowa State.

Things started to change in 1968 when then-Iowa athletic director Forest Evashevski announced that series would be renewed, beginning in 1977. The media didn't pay much attention to it then because the renewal was still nearly a decade away.

Iowa officials still were reluctant to renew the series because they feared what might happen, from riots in the stands to fights on the field.

But Iowa State officials continued to press the issue, insisting that a deal had been made. It eventually became a political football, as the State Board of Regents sent the matter to arbitration. After hearing both sides and reviewing the facts, the arbitrator ruled in Iowa State's favor.

So, after 42 years of being dormant, the series was renewed on September 17, 1977, in Iowa City.

The game didn't match the hype, though, as Iowa won a relatively boring affair 12–10 at Kinnick Stadium.

ABC was there to televise the game, which was played without incident.

Every game since the series was renewed has been sold out, and most have been televised to a regional audience.

And though fans from both schools despise losing this game, it doesn't mean the end to the season.

Iowa proved that in 1981 when it lost to Iowa State but went on to win the Big Ten title and play in the Rose Bowl.

Iowa also lost to Iowa State at home in heartbreaking fashion in 2002 but rebounded to finish undefeated in the Big Ten and 11-2 overall.

The Hawkeyes were leading 24-7 at halftime in Kinnick Stadium, but then lost the momentum early in the third quarter.

Iowa State scored 17 points in the third quarter on three Hawkeye fumbles and also had a safety. Iowa was outscored 23-0 in the third quarter and played from behind the rest of the way. Iowa fans looked on in disbelief as the eventual Big Ten champion collapsed at home. Many wondered if the 36-31 loss would ruin Iowa's season.

But Iowa State went on to struggle that season, while Iowa marched through the Big Ten slate undefeated and ultimately faced USC in the Orange Bowl.

One of the few blemishes on Kirk Ferentz's coaching resume is his 3-5 record against the Cyclones. Ferentz recorded his victories in 2003, 2004 and 2006.

His 2005 squad was nationally ranked a heavily favored against the Cyclones but still got whipped 23-3 in Ames. Iowa suffered a blow when junior quarterback Drew Tate left the game with a concussion in the second quarter.

The series now starts a new chapter with former Texas defensive coordinator Gene Chizik replacing McCarney as the Iowa State coach shortly after the 2006 season. He has a tough charge in attempting to reproduce his predecessor's success against the Hawkeyes.

The late 1970s saw the Cyclones in control of the series. Hayden Fry would change all that.

CRAWFORD

58

IOWA VS. PURDUE

Since 1981, Iowa has dominated the series with Purdue, leading 16-5-1 over that span.

Iowa trails 32-44-3

Hayden Fry fixed a lot of things as the Iowa coach, including the series with Purdue.

Iowa had lost 18 consecutive games against Purdue when Fry climbed aboard in 1979. Fry lost his first two games against the Boilermakers, including a 58-13 demolition in 1980, but the misery finally ended in 1981.

Iowa crushed Purdue 33-7 in 1981 and went on to play in the Rose Bowl that season. The Boilermakers bounced back the next season with a 16-7 victory at home, but Purdue didn't win another game in the series until 1992.

Iowa defeated Purdue nine consecutive times from 1983 to 1991, some by huge margins.

One of the closest and most important games occurred in 1985 when Iowa quarterback Chuck Long faced Purdue quarterback Jim Everett.

Iowa had just suffered its first loss of the season two weeks earlier at Ohio State and dropped from No. 1 in the rankings.

The scored was tied at 24-24 late in the fourth quarter when Long marched the Hawkeyes down the field. Rob Houghtlin capped the drive by making a game-winning field goal.

The series has been more competitive since Joe Tiller took over at Purdue in 1997, although Iowa has won the last three games dating back to 2004.

IOWA VS. MICHIGAN STATE

Iowa leads 19-17-2

Iowa and Michigan State have a history of playing in close, hard-hitting games.

Thirteen of the 16 games played from 1982 to 2001 were decided by a touchdown or less.

Perhaps the most memorable—at least for Iowa fans—was the 1985 classic won by Iowa 35-31 at Kinnick Stadium.

Iowa was ranked No. 1 in the nation at the time, but trailed late in the fourth quarter. Hawkeye quarterback Chuck Long marched the Iowa offense the length of the field, setting the stage for one of the greatest moments in school history.

On fourth down at the Michigan State 1-yard line, Long faked a handoff to running back Ronnie Harmon, but the Michigan State defenders all thought Harmon had the ball.

As they tackled Harmon, Long had the ball hidden on his right hip and ran untouched into the end zone. Long held the ball above his head as he crossed over the goal line to secure the victory at Kinnick Stadium.

Michigan State was also the opponent the day Iowa clinched its first Rose Bowl appearance under Hayden Fry in 1981.

Ohio State had done Iowa a huge favor by upsetting Michigan earlier in the day. Now all that stood in the way of Iowa winning the Big Ten and going to Pasadena were the Spartans.

The game was close in the first half, but then word spread about Michigan's loss to Ohio State.

Iowa dominated the second half and cruised to a 36-7 victory at Kinnick Stadium.

Roses fell from the press box as fans celebrated Iowa's first Big Ten title in more than two decades.

During running back Owen Gill's four years in Iowa City, the Hawkeyes won three of four against Michigan State.

In 1990, the Hawkeyes won a 24–23 thriller in the Big House.

IOWA VS. MICHIGAN

Michigan leads 40–10–4

Nobody will ever mistake the Iowa-Michigan rivalry for the Michigan-Ohio State rivalry, but the Hawkeyes have had some of their greatest moments in football at the expense of the Wolverines. Iowa was ranked No. 1 in the nation when it defeated second-ranked Michigan 12–10 in 1985. Michigan native Rob Houghtlin made a 29-yard field goal as time expired to lift the Hawkeyes to the victory. Many Iowa fans still consider that the greatest moment in the history of the football program.

The victory in 1985 came a year after Iowa had shut out Michigan 26–0 at home. That was only the second time Michigan had been held scoreless in the series, which dates back to 1900.

Iowa also recorded back-to-back victories over Michigan in 2002 and 2003 under Coach Kirk Ferentz. The 34–9 victory in 2002 was stunning for a number or reasons, mostly because it was played at Michigan Stadium.

Hayden Fry defeated Michigan four times while coaching at Iowa. The first time was a 9–7 victory in 1981 that helped propel the Hawkeyes to the Rose Bowl for the first time in 23 years. The 1984 season marked the only time under Fry that Iowa defeated Michigan without playing in the Rose Bowl. Michigan has since gained revenge by winning the last three games in the series. The Wolverines defeated Iowa 23–20 in overtime in 2005 to snap Iowa's 22-game winning streak at Kinnick Stadium.

The series is still one-sided in terms of overall wins and losses, but it's certainly more competitive than when it first started. Michigan won 15 of the first 18 games in the series, including a 107–0 victory in 1902.

Talkin' Hawkeye Football

We thought we'd go straight to the source and let some of Iowa's greatest legends—and others with a unique perspective—share their thoughts about Hawkeye football. They put it much better than we could.

"I am so glad you could speak enthusiastically of your visit to Iowa City. *That little town means so much to me...It is almost like home. I love the people, the campus, the trees, everything about it. And it is beautiful in the spring...And I hope you strolled off across the golf course just at twilight and felt the peace and quiet of an Iowa evening, just as I used to do."*

—EXCERPT OF A LETTER FROM NILE KINNICK TO A FRIEND; IT WAS THE LAST LETTER HE EVER WROTE.

"The University of Iowa and the football coaching staff, *during my career, concentrated on football players as a whole person, not just as an athlete. They made sure we understood that college was meant for getting an education and earning your degree, not just going to bowl games."*

—QB CHUCK HARTLIEB, 1987 ACADEMIC ALL-AMERICAN, AND 1987 AND 1988 ALL-BIG TEN QUARTERBACK

***"I owe all of my success at the University of Iowa** and in the NFL to Coach Ferentz and Coach Fry. Kirk was an excellent technician, teacher and motivator. His knowledge of the game, and especially of offensive line play, was a great benefit to me and my career, and his expertise will assure future success for Iowa's offensive linemen."*

—FORMER ALL-PRO OFFENSIVE LINEMAN JOHN ALT

***"It's one of the biggest plays** and one of the best games in history. Hopefully, it's on ESPN Classic so one day I can sit back and tell my kids about it."*

—IOWA DEFENSIVE BACK JOVON JOHNSON, ON THE 2005 CAPITAL ONE BOWL

***"I don't think you could write a better script.** Nobody would believe it if you did."*

—IOWA COACH KIRK FERENTZ AFTER THE CAPITAL ONE BOWL

***"I couldn't get that answer** and then I looked up and saw Warren Holloway scoring the touchdown. The next thing I know, I'm on the bottom of a 10,000-pound pile. It was unbelievable."*

—IOWA DEFENSIVE BACK SEAN CONSIDINE ON ASKING HIS TEAMMATES ABOUT KYLE SCHLICHER'S FIELD-GOAL RANGE

***"Shucks, we didn't even need that last safety.** We just wanted to make it decisive."*

—IOWA LINE COACH JIM HARRIS AFTER A 4–0 VICTORY AT PURDUE IN 1939

Kirk Ferentz

Drew Tate

"I'm not a big guy or anything like that. *When I'm out nobody walks up and says anything to me. It's probably because they don't recognize me, but that's OK. I get enough exposure to everything like that. I don't need to go out and do anything more."*

—IOWA QUARTERBACK DREW TATE ON LIVING LIFE IN THE MEDIA SPOTLIGHT

"The team's been through a lot this whole year, *and we've done a great job with everything we've had to conquer. We're doing a great job of winning, still playing for each other and still playing for the team."*

—DREW TATE, NOVEMBER 2004

"An excellent victory deserves one day, *and an extraordinary one deserves two."*

—UNIVERSITY PROVOST HARVEY DAVIS ADVISING STUDENTS THAT THERE WOULD BE TWO ADDITIONAL DAYS OF CHRISTMAS VACATION IN HONOR OF THE 1957 ROSE BOWL VICTORY

"Believe me, I'm daunted by the task *of having to move forward and hire a guy to come into the considerably cold shadow behind Hayden Fry. This is not going to be an easy task for whoever ends up with the job because the standard that [Fry] set is a very, very high standard indeed."*

—FORMER IOWA ATHLETIC BOB BOWLSBY COMMENTING AT FRY'S RETIREMENT PRESS CONFERENCE

THE WISDOM OF HAYDEN FRY

***"I have no time schedule** on getting Iowa a winning football team. But I will tell you we will be competitive, tough and colorful. If I did not believe Iowa could win in the near future, I would not have left North Texas."*

—FRY UPON BEING INTRODUCED AS THE NEW IOWA COACH ON DECEMBER 9, 1978.

***"We have only one place to go and that's up.** I have been extremely impressed with the people from this institution who have told me they want a winning team. I have done my homework to see that Iowa will make the commitment needed to have a winning team and I have been assured this will be done."*

—MORE FROM FRY'S DECEMBER 9, 1978 PRESS CONFERENCE.

***"We have to have an equal opportunity.** Our stick has to be as long as the sticks being used by those we play."*

—HAYDEN FRY

***"To say this will be an easy job would be crazy.** A lot of my fellow coaches will probably think I am crazy for leaving the security of North Texas. But I want the opportunity to take a place that is not recognized as a football factory and make it successful. A lot of people like to climb mountains. I like to take football teams and turn them into winners. If I don't make it here, I will have no one but myself to blame."*

—HAYDEN FRY, DECEMBER 9, 1978

"Adios."

—FRY'S LAST WORD AT HIS RETIREMENT PRESS CONFERENCE WHEN ASKED IF HE HAD ANYTHING ELSE TO SAY TO REPORTERS

"First we get our butts kicked. *Then we get complimented. I just told the team that if I see one single man with a smile on his face, I'll bust him in the mouth. Losing is losing and we didn't play well. These kids have been babied and pampered so much when they lose that it makes me sick. Losing and looking good is a bunch of crap."*

—HAYDEN FRY AFTER A 21-6 LOSS TO OKLAHOMA IN 1979

"The best recruiting job *we've ever done was getting Chuck Long to come back for that fifth year."*

—IOWA COACH HAYDEN FRY ON LONG'S DECISION TO RETURN FOR THE 1985 SEASON

"What a fantastic football game. *Whew, I feel like I've been run over by a truck. I think the good Lord was smiling on us today."*

—FRY AFTER THE 35-31 VICTORY OVER MICHIGAN STATE IN 1985

"I'll remember this group *for all the great things they've accomplished. These seniors have brought great recognition and exposure to the University of Iowa and the entire state. As of right now, I'd have to say this is my No. 1 victory, the finest ever. It's a great day for the state of Iowa."*

—FRY'S COMMENTS AFTER IOWA DEFEATED MINNESOTA 31-9 IN THE 1985 REGULAR-SEASON FINALE TO CLINCH THE BIG TEN TITLE AND ROSE BOWL BERTH.

"As you can see this is very difficult for me. *It's the only thing I've ever done. But I've got good reasons for doing it now."*

—FRY'S PRESS CONFERENCE ANNOUNCING HIS RETIREMENT ON NOVEMBER 23, 1998

NILE KINNICK'S UNIVERSITY OF IOWA COMMENCEMENT SPEECH

May 20, 1940

The remarks I have to make tonight are very brief, but nonetheless, with your permission, I am going to read them rather than attempt to render them without the benefit of a text. I prepared this short talk several weeks ago, but since then, so many events of terrible and ominous significance have taken place in the world that I almost revised it. The bloody holocaust raging in Europe with its possible repercussions in this country tends to exert depressive influence on all of us, and as a result, many of you will scoff at many of my remarks as foolish hopes and mere fictions. However, whether we know it or not, or like it or not, we in this country live by idealistic hopes and by fictions. And it may be that in the last analysis these seeming fictions and idealisms will prove to be the only realities. With this thought in mind, I shall read this speech with absolutely no apologies for the hopes and aspirations expressed.

Tonight, we seniors are gathered here as college graduates. Four short but dynamic years have gone fleeing by. It seems only yesterday that we entered this university as the very greenest of freshmen. Each one of us has treated and experienced these four years in different ways. To some, it has been one grand holiday at father's expense marred only by the necessity of a certain amount of study and classroom attendance. To others, it has been a grand opportunity to fulfill the hopes and aspirations of posterity-minded parents. And to still others, it has been a stern and intense experience—an opportunity, yes—but realized on only by treading the rough and rocky road of unmitigated hard work. I speak of you courageous boys and girls unfavored by financial assistance from home, who have earned your way by outside work on this campus, who have struggled desperately to meet your physical needs and at the same time maintain a decent classroom average. No social activities or frivolous pleasures have been yours, but you have asked for no quarter nor given any. You have been willing to pay the price for that which so many of us take as a matter of course. You hold your heads high tonight and rightly so, for you have fought and won.

But regardless of what this college experience has meant to different students, this evening we stand as one body, and in a few days, we shall stand together once more to receive that which is emblematic of four years of academic study well done—our diploma. Some of us will treasure this scrap of paper, some will be indifferent, and some will be cynical and unappreciative. But to all of us, it will serve as a sort of union card; hence forward, we are members of that great group who have "been to college." Unfortunately, it can't honestly be said that we are now educated, but certainly, at least, this diploma indicates that we have been satisfactorily exposed to the process.

And what now—where do we go from here? Certainly, it isn't a very pretty picture: unemployment and uncertainly here at home and international anarchy abroad. What part are we to play in this dynamic, ever-changing world? We are told on the one hand by the pedagogues of the university that the salvation of this nation is on our shoulders, and on the other hand depicted in the honorable Ding Darling's cartoons as naive, intellectually doped youngsters, without any ideas of practicality. But be that as it may, I know that we are full of ambition, courage, and a desire to do well for ourselves and for the society of which we are a part. We shall struggle to be sufficient unto the need. If it means better government, we shall be active there; if it means more enlightened business leadership, we shall strive for that; and if it means a broader, more responsible international outlook, count on us to be alert and ready.

Are we capable of successfully meeting the problems that face us? Have we been adequately equipped to fulfill our manifest duties and obligations? Only time can honestly answer. But we may be sure that if this great university is succeeding in her aims, then we shall be successful in ours. Fundamentally, all true education is composed of mental discipline and inspiration, and one is of no avail without the other. All successful teaching must hinge on these two necessary fundamentals. Nobly have our professors endeavored to embody these principles in their lectures and personal associations with us. Hopefully, now they will watch our progress to see if we make use of the tools with which they have tried to provide us.

However, the successful use of what we have learned here will be contingent entirely upon the addition of another element, which we alone can provide. For whether we realize it or not, we have lived a rather sheltered life here at the university. Here, our ideals are lauded, appreciated and protected; the development and expression of a social consciousness has been easy. But you know and I know that this period of easy idealism is now at an end. And it is here that this other element of which I speak and which can be provided by the individual and the individual alone enters into the picture.

I refer, fellow graduates, to a real, positive, mental courage. We all seem to have the courage to face the physical forces of life—sickness, poverty, unemployment, even war itself—but how about courage of conviction, of morality, of idealism, courage of faith in a principle tangible proof of which is slow in appearing? Herein lies that phase of these problems which we must meet by ourselves, unaided by any university-given tools. Here is that angle of the greater difficulty, which most often has proven the weak point in graduates of the past. True, we must learn to face adversity with equanimity, and even philosophically, but at the same time never for a moment losing sight of the ultimate goal, never failing in our ambition or our ideals. By now, we should have learned that success and happiness and attainment come only periodically, not permanently, that they really are only passing moments in our experience, and that therein lies the explanation of the law of progress and human dynamics. By now, we should realize that the battle is life itself, and that our joy and happiness should lie as much in the struggle to overcome as in the fruition of a later day.

So let us confidently take courage in what we deem to be right, and, no matter what our line or endeavor may be, cling to its concomitants of persistence, desire, imagination, hope, and faith. Our competitive urge must not only be objective but subjective, not only physical but spiritual. Injustice, oppression, and war will ultimately bring on their own destruction; suffering and misery eventually awaken the human race. But that is the long, sad, unenlightened road we have taken in the centuries past. Now is the time for these problems to be solved by enlightened thought and understanding. We can accomplish much if we implement mental discipline and inspiration with real mental courage. The task is not easy; wishful thinking will not do the job. We shall have to battle until we seemingly have reached the end of the line, then tie a knot and hang on. This is not just a figure of speech but an imperative necessity.

IOWA

Traditions and Pageantry

What is a college football Saturday without the pageantry? When it comes to the traditions and experiences that make college football so unique—unlike any other sport—the University of Iowa takes a back seat to no other school in the country.

Here's a small sample of what makes Iowa football unique.

THE FANS

Any discussion of Iowa's tradition has to start with the fans, because their devotion is unmatched by most schools.

Iowa earned a spot in the 2006 Alamo Bowl despite finishing 6–6 overall and losing five of the last six regular-season games. The Hawkeyes got the nod mostly because their fans have a reputation for flocking to bowl games and spending lots of money to support the team.

"Based on their past visits and the leadership of Kirk Ferentz we anticipate the Riverwalk will be a sea of black and gold with the legions of Hawkeye fans coming to San Antonio to support their team," said Bob Cohen, Alamo Bowl Chairman.

Cohen's prediction proved accurate as more than 10,000 Iowa fans attended the Alamo Bowl in San Antonio.

Iowa has had incredible support at the Rose Bowl, with as many as 30,000 fans making the trip west to Pasadena.

A similar number also traveled south to Miami for the 2003 Orange Bowl.

Kinnick Stadium, which has a seating capacity of around 70,000, sells out on a regular basis for home games and just recently went through a $90 million renovation project. The renovations were aimed at making things more convenient for fans on game day.

Iowa annually ranks among the top 25 programs in the nation in home attendance and has sold out every home game for the past four seasons.

Hayden Fry noticed the fans' enthusiasm while watching tape of Iowa play as he mulled over taking the job in 1978. Fry couldn't believe how excited the fans got just when Iowa made a first down.

"Imagine what they'll do if we score a touchdown," Fry joked at the time.

Fry paid tribute to the Iowa fans after the Hawkeyes clinched a spot in the Rose Bowl in 1981. Iowa hadn't been to the Rose Bowl in 23 years and hadn't had a winning season in 19 years.

"Among the people I feel happiest for are those loyal Iowa fans who have been denied for so long," Fry said. "I'd say those people were a great motivating factor to our players this season. What other fans in the country would stick with a losing program for so long? It's the wildest thing I've ever seen."

Iowa is the only state with a Big Ten school that doesn't have a professional sports team or two competing for the fans' interest. The Hawkeyes are never short on attention or fan support.

THE SWARM

Hayden Fry left his mark on the Iowa football program in many ways, including how the team takes the field on game day. Unlike most college teams whose players rush on to the field, the Iowa players hold hands and jog together in a group called the Swarm. Fry created the Swarm as a way to promote togetherness among the players. Former Fry assistant Kirk Ferentz has kept the swarm since becoming the Iowa coach in 1999.

HAYDENISMS

Fry had a unique way of expressing himself with his choice of words and his west Texas drawl. He coined a number of catch phrases that became known as Haydenisms. One of the more popular phrases was "scratch where it itches," which basically means you attack an opponent's weakness. Fry also referred to an injured player as having a "hitch in his get-along," or as being "buggered up." Fry used the phrase "an old mule with blinders on," to explain that he was focused solely on coaching.

IOWA'S UNIFORMS

There is a reason why Iowa's black-and-gold uniform resembles the look of the Pittsburgh Steelers. Hayden Fry copied the Steelers' look after being hired at Iowa in 1979. Pittsburgh was the dominant NFL team at the time and Fry wanted to project a winning attitude.

Iowa's uniform has gone through some changes over the years, but it still bears that resemblance to the Steelers' uniform.

IOWA'S TIGER HAWK LOGO

Fry felt that marketing the Iowa football program was a major part of rebuilding it. He helped introduce the tiger hawk logo, which is now synonymous with Iowa athletics. The tiger hawk is a cartoonish version of a hawk in profile.

THE HAWKEYES/HERKY THE HAWK

Iowa's nickname dates back to 1838 and was originally applied to a hero in the fictional novel *The Last of the Mohicans,* written by James Fenimore Cooper. Author Cooper had the Delaware Indians bestow the name on a white scout who lived with them.

The Hawkeye nickname gained a recognizable symbol in 1948 when a cartoon character later to be dubbed Herky the Hawk was hatched. The creator was Richard Spencer III, instructor of journalism. The hawk was an immediate hit and acquired the nickname through a statewide contest held by the UI athletic department. John Franklin, a Belle Plane, Iowa, native and a UI graduate, was the person who suggested Herky.

Herky has come to symbolize Iowa athletics. He even donned a military uniform during the Korean War and became the insignia for the 124th Fighter Squadron.

During the 1950s, Herky came to life as the mascot for football games. Herky now can be seen at most Iowa sporting events.

ALLIANT ENERGY

NEXT MAN IN

That phrase has been made popular during Iowa's recent rise to national prominence under Kirk Ferentz. It means that you make do with the players you have. If somebody is unable to perform, the next man in is expected to pick up where the starter left off.

KINNICK STADIUM

Iowa's home stadium opened in 1929 and just recently went through a $90 million renovation project. With a seating capacity of 70,585, Kinnick Stadium ranks as one of the 25 largest collegiate-owned stadiums in the nation.

It was originally called Iowa Stadium, but was renamed Kinnick Stadium in 1972 after former Heisman Trophy winner Nile Kinnick.

HAWKEYES

THE IOWA MARCHING BAND

The Iowa marching band was created about eight years before the school started a football program. It didn't take long for the marching band to become a part of the game-day atmosphere that still thrives today.

It's hard to picture an Iowa football game without the marching band performing before kickoff and during halftime.

The Iowa marching band is the oldest musical organization at the university with roots that trace back to 1880. For more than half of those years the band was under the direction of the military department.

Athletics were growing in popularity across the UI campus late in the 19th century, and the marching band was asked to play a benefit concert for the football team in February of 1894.

In 1905, the band appeared with the Glee Club at a celebration following a victory over Iowa State.

In 1911, the band raised enough money through student subscriptions and by other means to finance a trip to Minneapolis. However, Minnesota crushed Iowa 56–7, causing some to wonder if the band was a jinx.

By 1925, the band had more than doubled in size from 50 members to 125, all male. Ten years later two bands were formed for the first time. One was the concert band and the second was the varsity or sports band.

The band traveled by train during the early years, and it became open to women during World War II. In fact, former band director Charles B. Righter estimated that there were about 75 women and 25 men in the band during a period from 1942–1945.

After the war, the women in the band were allowed to remain as members until graduation if they so desired. But after that, the band returned to being an all-male organization.

It stayed that way until 1972 when two women were admitted to the marching band. Today band membership is about 50 percent men and 50 percent women.

PAUL W. BRECHLER PRESS BOX

THE SCOTTISH HIGHLANDERS

The Scottish Highlanders faded from the Iowa football scene in the early 1980s, but not before establishing a proud and unique legacy.

The Scottish Highlanders were established at the University of Iowa in 1937 when Col. George Dailey, head of the UI Military Department, organized the first college bagpipe unit in the United States.

It started as an all-male organization but eventually turned into an all-female band to compensate for the demands of World War II.

By 1942, there were 78 men in the bagpipe band. They dressed in knee socks and Scottish kilts and performed at most of the football games.

However, by the fall of 1943, 72 of the 78 band members had been called to serve in World War II. Most figured the bagpipe band would cease to exist until after the war.

But Pipe Major William Anderson had a different idea. He issued a call for women to help and the response was overwhelming as 160 women attended the tryout.

The all-female band became so popular that it stayed that way after World War II. At its peak, the Highlanders numbered in the 80s.

The band performed in 44 different states and throughout Britain before being disbanded in the early 1980s.

FLOYD OF ROSEDALE

A bet in 1935 between Minnesota Governor Floyd B. Olson and Iowa Governor Clyde Herring gave birth to Floyd of Rosedale. Floyd is the bronze statue of a pig that goes to the winning team in the series.

The bet was made in an effort to relieve tensions between the two schools. Iowa fans were upset with how star halfback Ozzie Simmons, an African-American, had been treated by the Minnesota players in the 1934 game. Simmons was one of the few black players in the Big Ten at the time.

After Iowa lost the 1935 game, Olson presented Floyd of Rosedale, a full-blooded champion pig and brother of BlueBoy from Will Rogers' movie, *State Fair*. Olson gave the pig to the University of Minnesota and commissioned St. Paul sculptor Charles Brioscho to capture Floyd's image.

Floyd is 21 inches long and 15 inches high. The winning school is entitled to keep Floyd on campus until it loses the annual border battle.

THE CY-HAWK TROPHY

The Cy-Hawk Trophy was created when Iowa and Iowa State resumed their rivalry in 1977. The Des Moines Athletic Club donated a trophy to be awarded to the winner of the annual instate battle. The trophy features a football player carrying a ball in his left hand and uses a stiff arm with his right arm. A likeness of Herky the Hawk and Cy the Cardinal also are on the front of the trophy.

THE HEARTLAND TROPHY

The Heartland Trophy was introduced in 2004 and goes each year to the winner of the Iowa-Wisconsin game. The trophy was designed and crafted by artist and former Iowa player Frank Strub. The trophy, which is a bull mounted on a walnut base, has been inscribed with all the scores of the games in the series.

GREATER DES MOINES
ATHLETIC CLUB
THE CY - HAWK
TROPHY
IOWA
40
HAWKEYES
GOPHERS
72

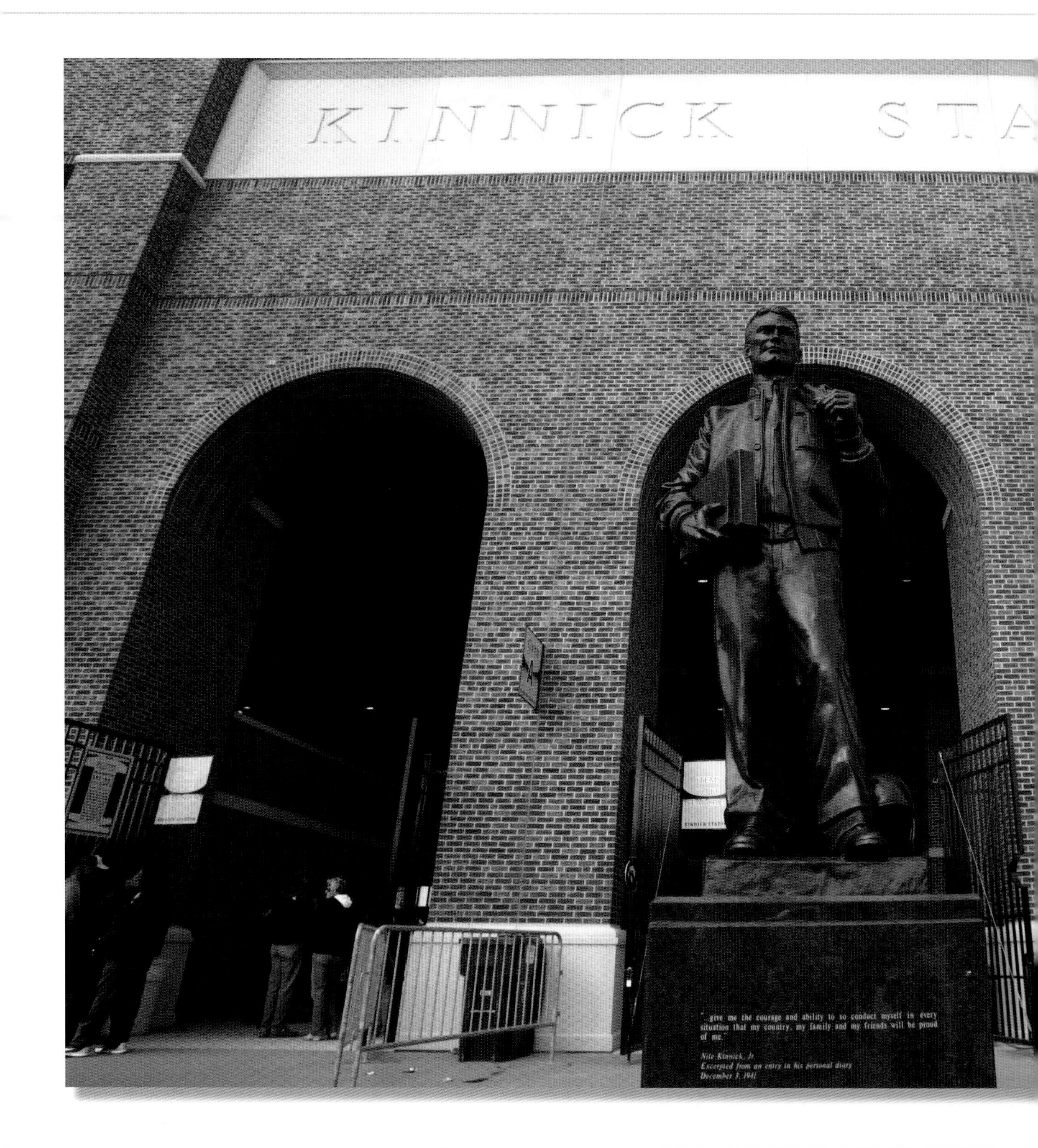
KINNICK STA
"...give me the courage and ability to so conduct myself in every situation that my country, my family and my friends will be proud of me."
Nile Kinnick, Jr.
Excerpted from an entry in his personal diary
December 1, 1941

THE VISITOR'S PINK LOCKER ROOM

Hayden Fry was a psychology major in college, which explains why the visitor's locker room at Kinnick Stadium was painted pink.

Fry always looked for a mental edge. And since pink is supposed to have a calming effect, he had the walls in the visitor's locker room painted that color.

Former Michigan coach Bo Schembechler became so obsessed with the pink walls that he had his assistant coaches buy white paper to cover them up on the morning of a game.

Iowa just recently completed a $90 million stadium renovation, but the new visitor's locker room was painted pink in Fry's honor.

RETIRED NUMBERS

At Iowa, the numbers 24 and 62 stand out, because no player has worn either one for more than a half century. They are the only retired numbers in the history of program. The No. 24 was worn by Nile Kinnick and No. 62 by Calvin Jones. Kinnick was a star halfback and defensive back for the 1939 Ironmen squad. He is the only player in school history to win the Heisman Trophy, and Iowa's stadium was named after him in 1972. Kinnick died in the Caribbean Sea in a crash of his fighter plane while on a training flight on June 2, 1943.

Jones was one of the most intimidating linemen to play at Iowa. He made 22 All-America teams in college and made first-team All-Big Ten three times. Jones also died in a plane crash on December 9, 1956.

Dallas Clark

IOWA'S WALK-ON LEGACY

Iowa's success with walk-ons was never more apparent than in the 2003 NFL draft. Iowa had five players selected in the first five rounds. Three of the five players—tight end Dallas Clark, center Bruce Nelson and defensive back Derek Pagel—were walk-ons at Iowa.

Iowa is believed to be the only school to ever have three former walk-ons selected in the same NFL draft.

Hayden Fry relied heavily on walk-ons as the Iowa coach, and now so does Kirk Ferentz. Recruiting is still an inexact science despite all the new technology. Some kids still fall under the radar, but need only an opportunity to excel. Iowa has a history of providing that opportunity to walk-ons.

THE ROSE BOWL

Iowa has a 2–3 record in the Rose Bowl, with both victories taking place in the 1950s under Coach Forest Evashevski. The Hawkeyes defeated Oregon State 35–19 in the 1957 Rose Bowl and defeated California 38–12 in the 1959 Rose Bowl.

Iowa lost all three Rose Bowl games it played in under Hayden Fry. Washington beat the Hawkeyes 28–0 in 1982; UCLA beat Iowa 45–28 in 1986; and Washington defeated Iowa 46–34 in 1991.

I WA

IOWA

THE IOWA FIGHT SONG

The name Meredith Wilson probably isn't recognizable to most Iowa football fans, but one of the songs she wrote is known by almost everybody. Wilson wrote the "Iowa Fight Song" that is sung at all sporting events. The song was aired nationwide for the first time on New Year's Eve 1951 on the annual production of NBC radio's "The Big Show" from New York City. It was introduced in Iowa City six weeks later when it was played by the Iowa band at halftime of the Iowa-Indiana basketball game on February 12, 1951. Hawkeye fans have been singing the song at sporting events ever since.

The word is "Fight! Fight! Fight! for IOWA,"

Let every loyal Iowan sing;

The word is "Fight! Fight! Fight! for IOWA,"

Until the walls and rafters ring (Go Hawks!)

Come on and cheer, cheer, cheer, for IOWA

Come on and cheer until you hear the final gun.

The word is "Fight! Fight! Fight! for IOWA,"

Until the game is won.

ALL
ABOUT
MICHIGAN

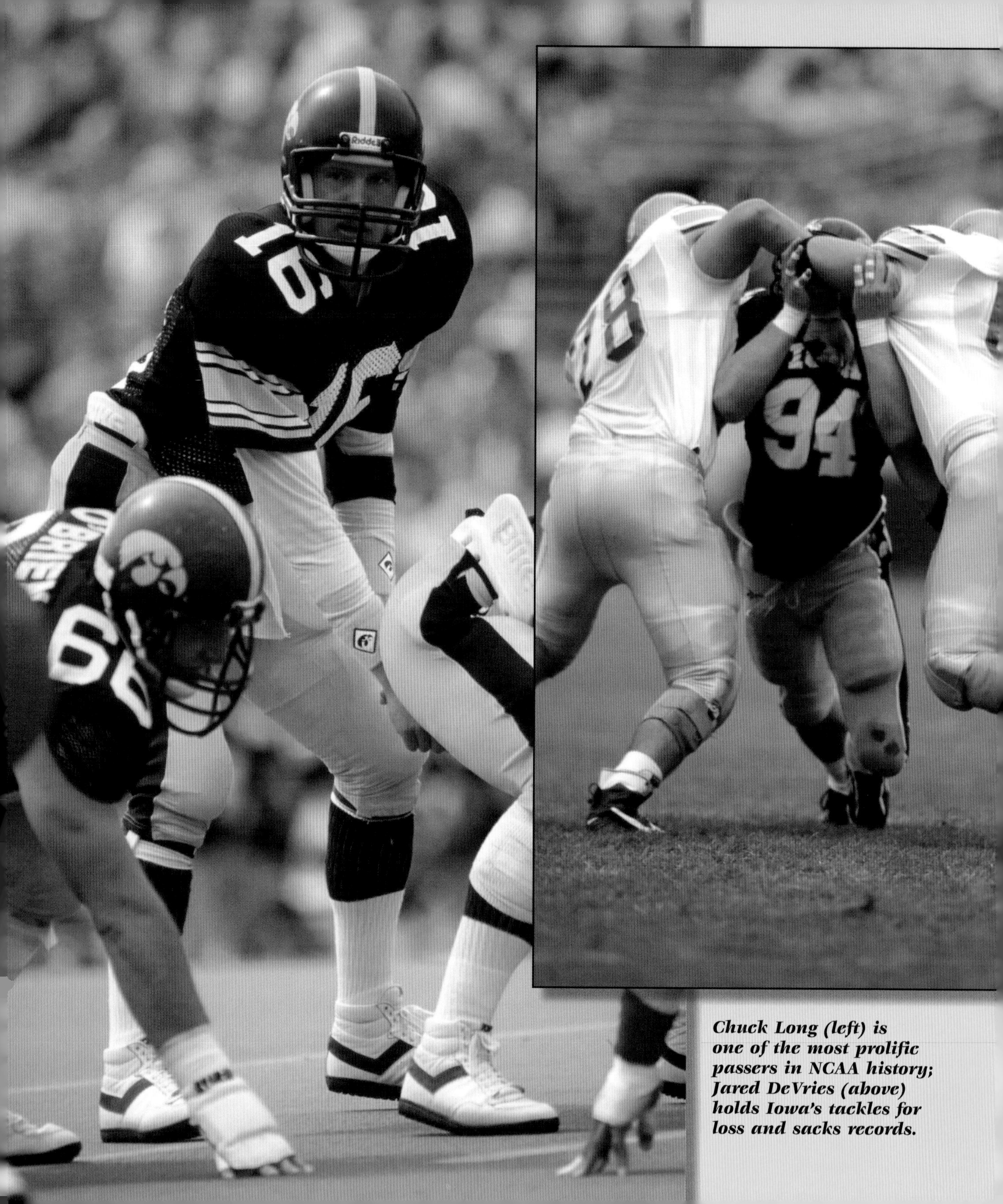

Chuck Long (left) is one of the most prolific passers in NCAA history; Jared DeVries (above) holds Iowa's tackles for loss and sacks records.

Facts and Figures

CAREER STATISTICAL LEADERS

- Rushes: 837, Sedrick Shaw
- Rushing yards: 4,156, Sedrick Shaw
- Rushing touchdowns: 33, Sedrick Shaw
- Yards per attempt: 5.9, Tavian Banks
- All-Purpose yards: 4,978, Ronnie Harmon
- Pass attempts: 1,203, Chuck Long
- Pass completions: 782, Chuck Long
- Passing yards: 10,461, Chuck Long
- Passing touchdowns: 74, Chuck Long
- Completion percentage: 65.0, Chuck Long
- Receptions: 157, Kevin Kasper
- Receiving yards: 2,271, Tim Dwight
- Receiving touchdowns: 21, Danan Hughes, Tim Dwight
- Total offense: 10,254, Chuck Long
- Tackles: 492, Larry Station
- Tackles for loss: 78, Jared DeVries
- Interceptions: 18, Nike Kinnick, Devon Mitchell
- Sacks: 42, Jared DeVries

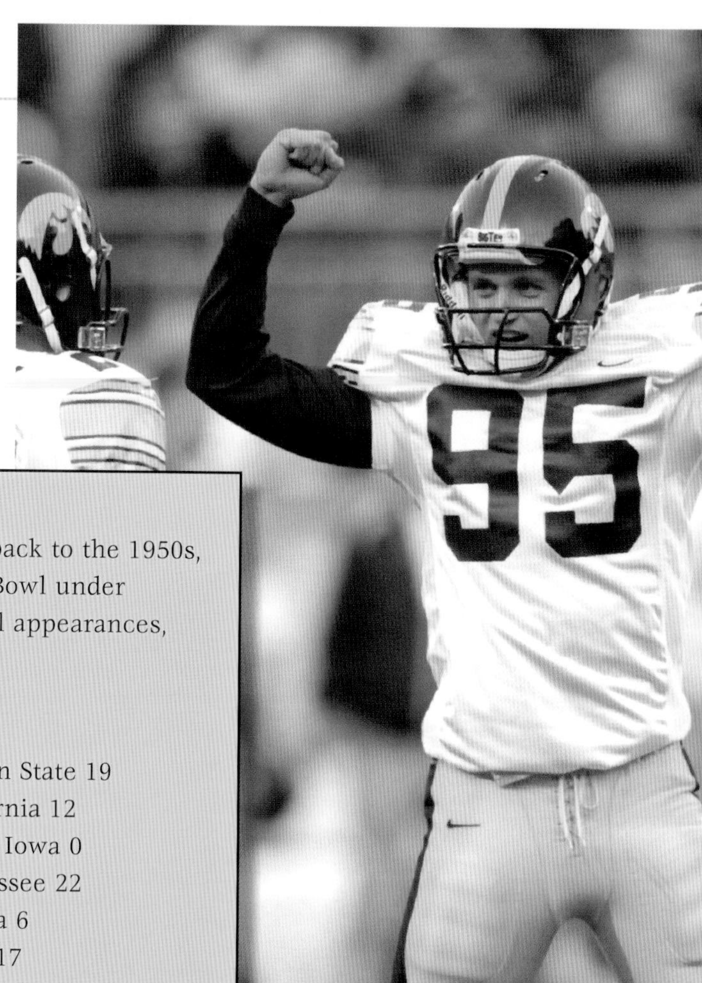

Nate Kaeding was a consensus All-American in 2003 and an integral part of the 2004 Outback Bowl.

BOWL TRADITION

Iowa has a rich bowl tradition that dates back to the 1950s, when the Hawkeyes twice won the Rose Bowl under Forest Evashevski. Iowa has made 22 bowl appearances, including 20 since 1981.

RECORD: 11–10–1

1957 Rose Bowl	Iowa 35, Oregon State 19
1959 Rose Bowl	Iowa 38, California 12
1982 Rose Bowl	Washington 28, Iowa 0
1982 Peach Bowl	Iowa 28, Tennessee 22
1983 Gator Bowl	Florida 14, Iowa 6
1984 Freedom Bowl	Iowa 55, Texas 17
1986 Rose Bowl	UCLA 45, Iowa 28
1986 Holiday Bowl	Iowa 39, San Diego State 38
1987 Holiday Bowl	Iowa 20, Wyoming 19
1988 Peach Bowl	North Carolina State 28, Iowa 23
1991 Rose Bowl	Washington 46, Iowa 34
1991 Holiday Bowl	Iowa 13, Brigham Young 13
1993 Alamo Bowl	California 37, Iowa 3
1995 Sun Bowl	Iowa 38, Washington 18
1996 Alamo Bowl	Iowa 27, Texas Tech 0
1997 Sun Bowl	Arizona State 17, Iowa 7
2001 Alamo Bowl	Iowa 19, Texas Tech 16
2003 Orange Bowl	Southern California 38, Iowa 17
2004 Outback Bowl	Iowa 37, Florida 17
2005 Capital One Bowl	Iowa 30, Louisiana State 25
2006 Outback Bowl	Florida 31, Iowa 24
2007 Alamo Bowl	Texas 26, Iowa 24

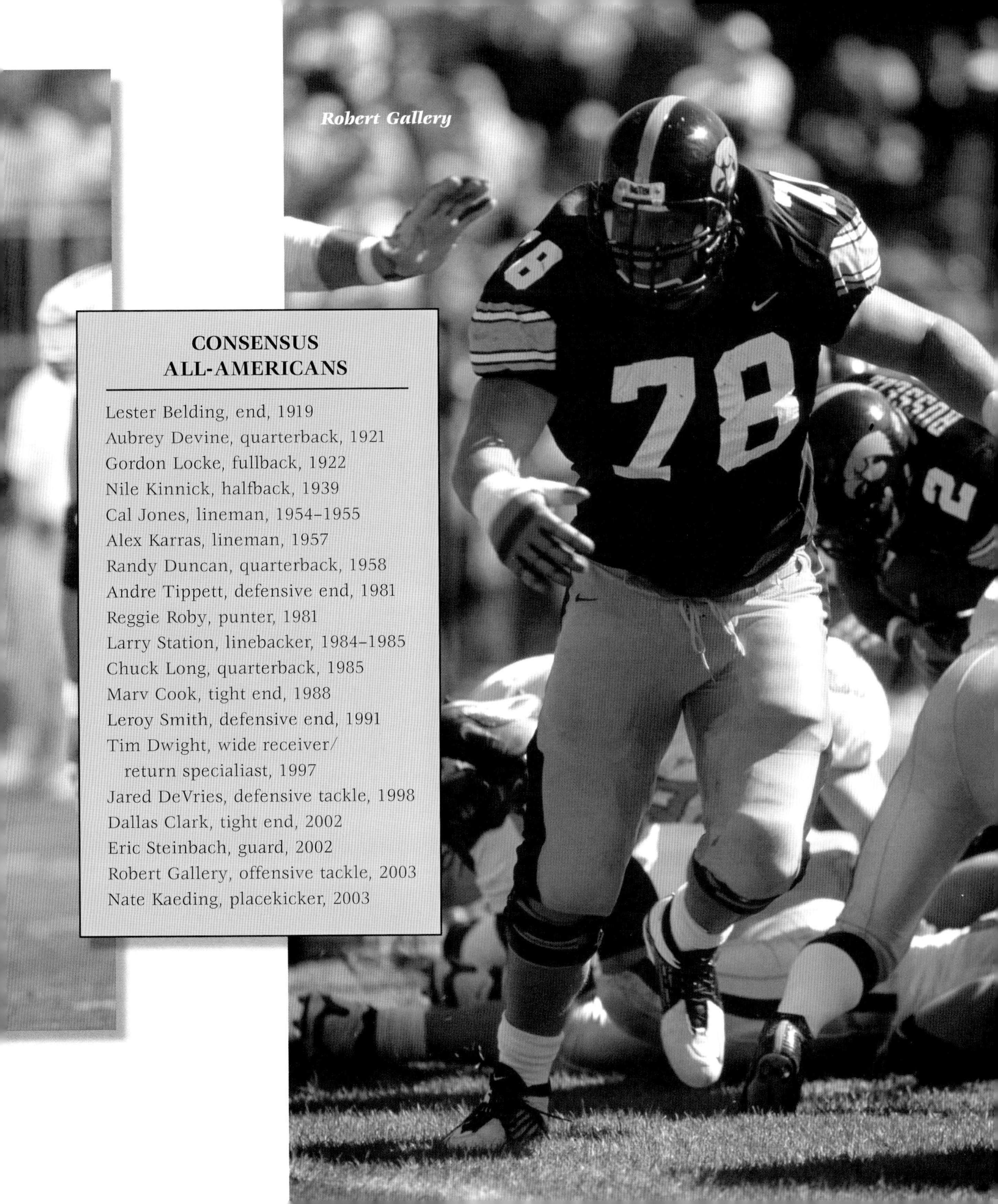

Robert Gallery

CONSENSUS ALL-AMERICANS

Lester Belding, end, 1919
Aubrey Devine, quarterback, 1921
Gordon Locke, fullback, 1922
Nile Kinnick, halfback, 1939
Cal Jones, lineman, 1954–1955
Alex Karras, lineman, 1957
Randy Duncan, quarterback, 1958
Andre Tippett, defensive end, 1981
Reggie Roby, punter, 1981
Larry Station, linebacker, 1984–1985
Chuck Long, quarterback, 1985
Marv Cook, tight end, 1988
Leroy Smith, defensive end, 1991
Tim Dwight, wide receiver/
return specialiast, 1997
Jared DeVries, defensive tackle, 1998
Dallas Clark, tight end, 2002
Eric Steinbach, guard, 2002
Robert Gallery, offensive tackle, 2003
Nate Kaeding, placekicker, 2003

Brad Banks

IOWA'S NATIONAL AWARD WINNERS

Heisman Trophy
Honoring the most outstanding college football player in the United States
Nile Kinnick, 1939

Other high finishers in Heisman Trophy voting:
Cal Jones, 10th in 1955
Kenny Ploen, ninth in 1956
Alex Karras, second in 1957
Randy Duncan, second in 1958
Chuck Long, seventh in 1984; second in 1985
Tim Dwight, seventh in 1997
Brad Banks, second in 2002

Outland Trophy
Honoring the outstanding interior lineman
Cal Jones, 1955
Alex Karras, 1957
Robert Gallery, 2003

Maxwell Award
Honoring the nation's outstanding college football player
Nile Kinnick, 1939
Chuck Long, 1985

Davey O'Brien Award
Honoring the No. 1 quarterback in the nation
Chuck Long, 1985
Brad Banks, 2002

AP National Player of the Year
Brad Banks, 2002

Lou Groza Award
Honoring the nation's top placekicker
Nate Kaeding, 2002

John Mackey Award
Honoring the nation's best tight end
Dallas Clark, 2002

Tim Dwight

HAWKEYES IN THE PRO FOOTBALL HALL OF FAME

Paul Krause, safety

Inducted 1998

Washington Redskins, 1964–1967;

Minnesota Vikings, 1968–1979

- Retired as NFL's all-time interception leader, with 81
- Played in eight Pro Bowls
- All-NFL four times
- Started at free safety in four Super Bowls for the Vikings

Emlen Tunnell, defensive back

Inducted 1967

New York Giants, 1948–1958;

Green Bay Packers, 1959–1961

- First African American elected to Pro Football Hall of Fame
- Key to Giants' famed "umbrella defense" of the 1950s
- Gained more yards (924) on interceptions and kick returns than the NFL rushing leader in 1952
- Retired as career leader in interceptions (79 for 1,282 yards) and punt returns (262 for 2,217 yards)
- Played in nine Pro Bowls
- All-NFL six times

HAWKEYES IN THE COLLEGE FOOTBALL HALL OF FAME

Name	Position	Years	Inducted
Dr. Eddie Anderson	Coach	1939–1944, 1946–1949	1971
Aubrey Devine	Halfback	1919–1921	1973
Randy Duncan	Quarterback	1956–1958	1997
Forest Evashevski	Coach	1952–1960	2000
Hayden Fry	Coach	1979–1998	2003
Calvin Jones	Offensive Lineman	1953–1955	1980
Howard Jones	Coach	1916–1923	1951
Alex Karras	Defensive Tackle	1956–1957	1991
Nile Kinnick	Halfback	1937–1939	1951
Gordon Locke	Fullback	1920–1922	1960
Chuck Long	Quarterback	1981–1985	1999
Fred "Duke" Slater	Lineman	1919–1921	1951